Kenneth Burke and Martin Heidegger

With a Note Against Deconstructionism

University of Florida Monographs
Humanities Number 60

D1600981

Kenneth Burke

&

Martin Heidegger

*With a Note
Against Deconstructionism*

Samuel B. Southwell

University Presses of Florida
University of Florida Press
Gainesville

Permissions to reprint material from various works quoted in this volume appear on pages 157–58.

B
945
.B774
S68
1987

Library of Congress Cataloging in Publication Data

Southwell, Samuel B.
  Kenneth Burke and Martin Heidegger—with a note against deconstructionism.

    (University of Florida humanities monograph; 60)
    Bibliography: p.
    Includes index.
    1. Burke, Kenneth, 1897– . 2. Heidegger,
Martin, 1889–1976. 3. Deconstruction. I. Title.
II. Series. University of Florida monographs.
Humanities; no. 60.
B945.B774S68 1987   111   87-10942
ISBN 0-8130-0872-7 (alk. paper)

For My Wife, Mary

Very few minds imagine even that the temple for "the unknown god" is going to receive on its steps, for the second time, some astonishing gospel—and yet isn't there some chance that the *necessary* idea of being will revive? Is not a boatsman, still soundlessly, approaching our nocturnal shore?

—Yves Bonnefoy

contents

Acknowledgments / ix

1. Introduction—Nietzsche: Burke, Heidegger / 1

2. Common Ground and "Being There" / 10

3. Burke's Act and Paradox of Being / 29

4. Being: The Later Heidegger / 42

5. The "Thing" and Questions of Faith / 58

6. Conclusion: The Necessary Metaphysics / 73

Appendix: Note Against Deconstructionism / 87
Jacques Derrida / 87
Paul de Man / 105

Notes / 133

Bibliography / 145

Index / 149

acknowledgments

I WISH to express my gratitude to the University of Houston for support making this book possible. The College of Humanities and Fine Arts and the Department of English have made time available by reducing my teaching responsibilities. The Research Council has provided funds for completion of the manuscript. Important improvements in the book have resulted from the advice of Raymond Gay-Crosier of the University of Florida, and from the excellent editing of the manuscript by the staff of the University Presses of Florida. A number of my colleagues have given me invaluable help—gifts of friendship which do not imply commitment to the positions I have argued here. The conception of the book arose from conversations with Timothy Crusius, of Texas A & M University. For reading the manuscript and helping me to improve it, I am indebted to Timothy Crusius, Justin Leiber, and Sherry Zivley, and, as always and in many things, to Irving Rothman. I am deeply appreciative of personal courtesies extended me by Kenneth Burke, whose work has contributed largely to my education. My largest debt is to Mary, to whom the book is dedicated.

chapter 1

Introduction—Nietzsche:
Burke, Heidegger

MOST OF what has occurred in the explosive development of critical theory in recent decades has been anticipated and often quite fully developed in the work of one man, Kenneth Burke. A revised Marxism, a revised Freudianism, hermeneutics, structuralism, semiotics, reader-response theory, theory of ritual, speech-act theory, even a kind of deconstructionism, and much else that is called postmodernism—it is all to be found in Burke, however improbable such an accomplishment may seem. We might seem to confront only the random play of an incredibly diverse genius, but there may also be something fundamental in Burke's thought that both truly holds it all together and makes it possible. That suggests a portentous possibility. It suggests that an area of seemingly inherent chaos and controversy can take on a measure of coherence and order. Any suggestion of synthesis is, of course, offensive to the most zealous advocates of postmodernism, but there must be an alternative to their scorched-earth cultural policy.

Efforts to define Burke's work often resort to triangulations with other writers who are more easily classifiable. My recourse will be a comparison between the thought of Burke and that of Martin Heidegger. I will attempt to demonstrate that such a procedure provides an optimal way of describing Burke's basic philosophical position and of showing its significance. The comparison will engender perspectives that may contribute also to our understanding of Heidegger.

The relevance of the general position shared by Heidegger and Burke will become increasingly clear as we come to realize that Jacques Derrida, as Arthur Clough said of Carlyle, has led us out into the desert and left us there. What we must say eventually about Derrida will determine in large part what we think about Heidegger and Burke. The central issue for Derrida as for Heidegger and Burke is the question of being, and his position is the diametrical opposite of theirs, despite Derrida's continual exploitation of the thought of Heidegger in the service of "deconstructionism." We are beginning now to understand that deconstructionism, like many aspects of postmodernist culture, is a last gasp of modernism in its nihilistic mode. The deconstructionists steadily disavow nihilism, but they do so on the basis of a faith the object of which eludes conceptual identification. The strategy of deconstructionism has thus its parallel in the anarchism of Prince Peter Kropotkin. It rests upon a faith that flowers will grow from the ashes of unrelieved negation, flowers of an as yet unknown variety. Accompanying this quaint faith are basic assumptions inherited from the older and outmoded avant-garde. Modernism, though it achieved affirmations, was a phenomenon of autonomous fragmentations stranded by their autonomies in time. The autonomy of language essential to deconstructionism is surely a last autonomy. For contemporary with the nihilism prevailing in most areas of art and culture that fly the postmodernist banner, there is a new and vitally integrative development, the only aspect of the culture distinctive of the postmodern period that can endure. It is a search for meaning in the interconnectedness of things and of the present with the past. A reorientation underway in all the human sciences has created a moment of experimentation with borrowed paradigms attended sometimes by chaos but redolent of new beginnings. Representative of the impulse toward unity and meaning is the work of Daniel Bell and Jürgen Habermas in which there is an assimilation of the most diverse areas of knowledge and in which Bell from the political right and Habermas from the left move toward a center. And we are now discovering the great Mikhail Bakhtin, for whom men are united in a linguistic-social continuum. There is everywhere a movement toward the consolidation of knowledge and of temporal continuities. It is such a goal that can be served by our reappropriating the thought of Kenneth Burke, remaining mindful of Heidegger's saying that history is "the 'recurrence' of the possible" and that an authentic culture is capable of "handing down to itself the possibilities it has inherited."

The profile of Burke that will emerge in a comparison with Heidegger can be further illuminated by reference to a number of other writers who, unlike Burke, have been directly influenced by Heidegger—Jean-Paul Sartre, Jacques Lacan, and especially Hans-Georg Gadamer, whose work is in large part an elaboration of Heidegger. The work of Ernst Cassirer bears some similarity to that of Burke, and both Gadamer and Cassirer can serve heuristic purposes, providing occasional shortcuts for the understanding of philosophical issues.

Some relatively superficial similarities between Burke and Heidegger are of interest. They are closely contemporary. Heidegger, who died in 1976, was born in 1889; Burke, still very much alive in 1987, was born in 1898. Both men in their youth were deeply religious. Both retain the impress of extensive theological reading. Both rejected urban life for the countryside. Both are notable for early, though very different, stands on National Socialism. Both are considered difficult writers; Heidegger is supremely difficult, and Burke is likely to repel the uninitiated. Very significantly, the paragraphs of both men are littered with words in quotation marks signaling the inadequacies of standard vocabularies for the tasks they undertake. Both men began in reaction against their intellectual heritages. There is about both men a kind of enormity, a radical extravagance. Heidegger's project was a single-handed effort to change the episteme of the West. In the labyrinth of history, culture, and language in which Burke labors, he seems to take on heroic dimensions as we come to understand that alone and independently he has achieved most of the implications of the centrality of language that a century has labored to reveal.

If the similarities are arresting, the differences are dramatic. Both men were deeply influenced and then disillusioned by national experiences, but these were conflicting experiences—National Socialism in Heidegger's case; the Marxism of the thirties in Burke's. Heidegger's reputation retains a perhaps permanent stain from his brief but emphatic allegiance to the Nazi party. Burke, in a review of *Mein Kampf*, was one of the first in America to warn of the dangers of Nazism.[1] Heidegger began his education in training for the priesthood at a Jesuit seminary. Burke's youthful religious experience was not a consequence of family tradition but a recourse of his own choice—and very American. He became for a time in his teens a Christian Scientist.[2] (Interestingly, in his old age a Roman Catholic priest is in regular communication with him, though apparently to no avail.)

Heidegger was quintessentially an academic being. He was for a time assistant at the University of Freiburg to Edmund Husserl, to whom his masterpiece *Being and Time* is dedicated.[3] He held his first chair at the University of Marburg, but later returned to Freiburg, where he served as rector. Burke attended briefly Ohio and Columbia universities, but took no academic degrees. He nevertheless spent most of his adult life on the faculty of one university or another, serving at one time as visiting professor of sociology at Harvard and eventually in a permanent appointment at Bennington College, from which he retired in 1961. Within universities, Heidegger was always an insider. Burke was an outsider, though his association with dominant academic critics of the thirties and forties was so close as to establish the persistent but thoroughly mistaken notion that he was a New Critic and one of the founders of that school of criticism.[4]

Intellectually, Burke and Heidegger are united by descent from a common ancestor to whom both are enormously indebted: Friedrich Nietzsche. A common profile of the three writers, comprehending fundamental aspects of their thought, may be constructed of the following propositions: (1) The dominant forces of modern thought are inimical to human wholeness. (2) Scientific-mathematical description of nature is meaningless. (3) Causal thinking must be avoided. (4) Determinism is a fiction. (5) Most of the philosophy of the past is made invalid by crucial error. (6) The source of error is to be found in Greek philosophy following the pre-Socratics. (7) The conceptions of "progress" and "liberalism" must be rejected. (8) The error of most modern thought is exacerbated by the Cartesian conception of "consciousness" as a unitary thing. (9) There is no subject-object dichotomy. (10) The subject is a multiplicity. (11) The power of language pervades and largely controls all human thought and all human perception. (12) All human thought and perception are necessarily interpretation (hermeneutics). (13) Beneath the interpreted world, there is no contrastingly real world; there is only an "abyss" (the development of the thought of both Heidegger and Burke requires that eventually this be qualified). (14) Not only must rationalism be rejected, but rational processes are inherently suspect. (15) Art is a more reliable guide to reality than is reason, and the rational (scientific-intellectual) paradigm of the world must be replaced by an artistic paradigm. (16) The metaphysics of the past must be replaced by a new metaphysics. (17) The new metaphysics will be an affirmation that will restore wholeness to life. (I use the term *metaphysics* in the broadest possible sense which recognizes materialism as metaphysics. The term used in Heidegger's special sense will always be in quotation marks.)

The debts of Heidegger and Burke to Nietzsche are both specific and conspicuous, and Nietzsche's influence on them survives the rejection by both men of large parts of his work. (Some of these influences will be indicated later in this study.) Indeed, Burke and Heidegger both write a kind of abstract, philosophical poetry which must be inspired by the poetry of Nietzsche. More importantly, when Burke and Heidegger describe the departures determining their basic intellectual projects they do so with reference to Nietzsche.

Heidegger says that "all the themes of Western thought, though all of them transmuted, fatefully gather together in Nietzsche's thinking." And, "With greater clarity than any other man before him, Nietzsche saw the necessity of change in the realm of essential thinking." Nietzsche, says Heidegger, "sees clearly that in the history of Western man something is coming to an end." Nietzsche is "the West's last thinker."[5] But Nietzsche's new beginning Heidegger deplores. In his four-volume work *Nietzsche*, Heidegger says, "*We must grasp Nietzsche's philosophy as the metaphysics of subjectivity.*" In the "metaphysics" of subjectivity "man is subject in the sense of the drives and affects present before us as the 'ultimate fact'; that is, in short, the *body*. In such recourse to the body as the metaphysical guideline, all world interpretation is pursued." Thinking that has the body as guideline is what Heidegger calls "valuative thinking," which is the "essence and fulfillment of the metaphysics of subjectivity." And: "Thinking in values veils the collapse of the essence of Being and truth." Hence, Heidegger's thought begins in understanding Nietzsche's thought and repudiating essential aspects of it: "The insight into these relationships was the impetus for the treatise *Being and Time*." Against Nietzsche, he declares, "The essence of man is determined by Being itself from the essence (understood verbally) of the truth of Being."[6] The "thinking of Being" is Heidegger's lifelong project; *Being and Time* is his central work and his masterpiece. His relationship to Nietzsche is a basic opposition.

In Burke's first discursive work, *Counter-Statement,* he formulates the orientation that will persist throughout his work: "And as for dignity, whatever kind of dignity survives will not be based on a theory of cosmic favoritism, but on a scheme of human potentialities, a conception of what man 'could be' (such a turn from metaphysical to psychological foundations as we have saluted in Nietzsche)."[7] There is for Burke a single constant, the body: "Insofar as the neurological structure remains constant, there will be a corresponding constance in the devices by which sociality is maintained." Therefore, "the essentials of purpose and gratification will not change."[8] Burke's thought, then, remains "valuative thought" in the tradition of Nietzsche, but his values are not Nietzsche's. His values—unquestionably shameless in a postmodernist world—are order, balance, coherence, dignity, and "wonder, resignation, tolerance, and sympathy."[9] His lifelong preoccupation is to preserve the power of human affirmation against the inroads of nihilism. He is temperamentally averse to the will-to-power and the Over-man. In these conceptions he sees what he calls the "technological psychosis." What he finds in Nietzsche "is perhaps the fullest, most self-contradictory symbolization of the transition from the pre-technological to the technological psychosis which mankind will ever possess. We might call it the 'pro-technological' attitude."[10] Heidegger's analysis is strikingly similar: "In the sense of Nietzsche's metaphysics, only the Over-man is appropriate to an absolute 'machine economy', and vice versa: he needs it for the institution of absolute dominion over the earth."[11] The exaltation of man in "dominion over the earth" violates Heidegger's crucial conception of the finitude of man. For Burke man remains the measure of whatever may be measured, but "the abyss" that lies beyond marks the finitude of man, which for both men results in a general attitude which Burke calls "piety."[12] For both men "technology" is a *bête noire* bred from tendencies inherent in the thought of the West.

Once Nietzsche's possibilities of affirmation have been rejected, what remains is his bequest of the incisive and pervasive nihilism that establishes a mordant need, response to which is definitive of the projects of Heidegger and Burke. Heidegger says, "People everywhere trace and record the decay, the destruction, the imminent annihilation of the world. . . . The world, men find, is not just out of joint but tumbling away into the nothingness of absurdity. Nietzsche who from his supreme peak saw far ahead of it all, as early as the eighteen-eighties, had for it the simple, because thoughtful words: 'The

Wasteland grows'."[13] The wasteland is in one of its aspects the default of meaning in science. "Physics," says Heidegger, "can make no assertions about physics."[14] The responses of Heidegger and Burke are efforts to establish on new grounds the concept of being, the devastation of which was Nietzsche's fundamental negation. "Being," says Cassirer, "is the foundation in which all meaning must ultimately be in some way grounded."[15] The recourse to being will be based on a conception of language that was also in large part an inheritance from Nietzsche.

Any approach to Heidegger and Burke should be informed by a special precaution. It concerns the charges of mysticism that have been brought against both men. The centrality of language to their thought is one ground for such caution, for there are homologies between religion and language. Cassirer explores a "unity of function" between "these two absolutely independent and unique forms," religion and language. He says, "The development of language is determined by its tendency to cling to the sensuous and yet strive beyond it, to surpass the narrow limits of the mere mimetic sign. And religion discloses the same characteristic opposition."[16] Burke says, "Everything that can be said about 'God' has its analogue in something that can be said about language."[17] In the course of demonstrating the linguistic (dialectic) origins of religion, Burke develops six analogies between language and religion, for instance, "the likeness between words about words and words about the Word." And: "Words are to nonverbal nature as Spirit is to Matter."[18] Burke recognizes in this a special danger: "Language being essentially a means of transcending brute objects, there is implicit in it the 'temptation' to come upon the idea of 'God' as the ultimate transcendence."[19] Partly in awareness of this, Burke anticipated the charge of mysticism, protesting that "anyone who would turn his skepticism against these vested interests of scientific rationalization" must "necessarily show some superficial affinity with religious rationalization" and "is suspected of a strong hankering to sink back into the Dark Ages of human thought."[20] Similarly Heidegger, at least in the early phase of the later work, protested repeatedly that the activity of the thinking of Being is remote from religion and that Being "is not God and not a cosmic ground."[21]

For the positivistic reader, however, there is a further problem. Thought conceived as autonomous must, in the modern world, tend strongly to exalt the authority of science, and, whether it does that or not, thought conceived as autonomous has but two choices: it must either eliminate God or it must become God, as it does in Hegel. For Nietzsche thought is not autonomous, but it is totally at the service of the will to power by which man can, in effect, make himself God. Heidegger and Burke, though in different ways, are deeply indebted to Hegel, as they are to Nietzsche, but they begin in reaction against both Hegel and Nietzsche. They begin by rejecting the autonomy of thought, of science, and of man. Thought which does not glorify man and rejects the final authority of thought and science cannot begin by eliminating God, though it will not necessarily conclude in the affirmation of God. The question of God must remain in abeyance, as it does for both Heidegger and Burke. So the question for the positivistic reader is whether or not he will permit the thought of Heidegger and Burke to begin at all. To permit it to begin is to commit oneself to the possibility of the development of a way of thinking that will find pervading things in general a principle or principles which do not submit to the mathematical descriptions of science. Such principles may be conceived as prior to the world described by science and as somehow larger than science and containing it as a derivative. Such principles might imply meaning in life, and they might bear resemblance to principles of systems of thought which are in fact theistic, but they may do this without being theistic. Indeed, it has been cogently argued that Hegel was an atheist.[22] If principles which engender meaning do not manifest personality and the inherently capricious power of deity, they may not fairly be dismissed by the word "mysticism" used as a stigma that would condemn all nonpositivistic thought. It may be of some value, however, to make a distinction between theistic mysticism and nontheistic mysticism. It will become clear that in Burke we do not find either kind of mysticism. Nor do we in the early Heidegger. I will leave pending for a while the question as to whether or not in the final development of the later Heidegger we observe a nontheistic mysticism.

In the character of the texts of both writers there is an extravagance, though the styles are markedly different. In Heidegger a kind of molten heat of concentration struggles with the subtleties of a project which even in the end remains elusive. In the writing of Burke there is a remarkable quality of diffusion in which everything leads to everything else in far-ranging concatenations, the profound consistency of which is fully realized only by the most careful study. Reading is made perilous by the fact that Burke's thought moves on a knife-edge between conflicting philosophical forces. The powerful personalities of both men submit language to constant distortion. The result is that both men have been repeatedly misunderstood, and attempting to treat both of them in a single, brief study may well seem foolhardy. Aware of the dangers, I have resorted in the following study to a massive use of quotations. Obviously this practice will not ensure the avoidance of error, but it can reduce error, and I think that in the case of such difficult writers it can be a service to the reader. The value of the practice will be most apparent in the treatment of *Being and Time,* where, for instance, a new term may be introduced thirty pages before it is defined. The almost insuperable difficulty of this text is to be accounted for, in part, by the way in which it is organized, and conceivably this may be explained by the fact that Heidegger published it before he had intended to, responding to a new policy on faculty publication.

In attempting to deal with a single aspect of so complex a writer as Burke, even if it is the central aspect, there is an additional danger of misleading. On that point I will feel some reassurance in the knowledge of the existence of Frank Lentricchia's *Criticism and Social Change,* which emphasizes Burke's wide-ranging heterogeneity.[23] Though I will quarrel with Lentricchia on a number of basic points, his is a brilliant and courageous work that illuminates and makes urgent certain aspects of Burke's contemporary relevance.

chapter 2

Common Ground and "Being There"

IN THE idea of the centrality of language, Burke and Heidegger come onto common ground, and they are very close to each other in their radical versions of this conception. The point requires close attention. I believe that clarity can best be achieved by constructing a hypothesis that will serve as a positivistic simulacrum of Heidegger's phenomenological description and as a reference point for identifying the positions of both men on the role of language. I will now attempt to construct in rough outline such a hypothesis based eventually on positivistic assumptions.

The argument might begin with Kant's famous statement: "Concepts without intuitions are empty; intuition without concepts is blind." Nelson Goodman is more emphatic: "Perception without conception is *blind* (totally inoperative)."[1] Concepts, according to Nietzsche, are "possible only when there are words."[2] All this is now to be translated into hypothetical biology. Concepts are word-memories; they are neurological phenomena that correspond directly to the sounds of words. That is, what we experience as a concept is the activation of an impress upon neuronal structures, the impress having resulted from the impact of the sound pattern of a word upon the tympanum of the ear. Striking implications now emerge. If seeing is always knowing, as Kant, Nelson Goodman, and many others have believed, then we can see only because we have language. The hypothesis assumes that non-human animals are, as Descartes maintained, automata. They neither see nor hear. Their auditory and visual systems are entirely operative and functional, but they are totally blind and deaf. Their sense organs are simply transfer systems for information which has as its only consequence the stimulation of, or the failure to stimulate, instinctive energies.

In the nonhuman brain, our hypothesis continues, sense organs have neuronal links only with triggering mechanisms of instinctive action. There are no neuronal links between the visual system and the auditory-vocal system. Either the neuronal connections are not there, or they have not been utilized. Such neuronal links are established, or utilized, when animal sounds begin to be referential, that is, when the neurological correlates of specific sound patterns come to have stable links with the neurological correlates of specific visual stimuli in a way that circumvents or modifies sense-instinct linkages. With the full development of language there are operative two memory systems, the auditory-motor system and the visual system, which exist in relations of constant retrieval and feedback to each other, a condition of constant recall, in one direction or the other.[3] This means that now every visual stimulus effects a potentiation of the auditory-vocal system. To the extent that this occurs, the visual stimulus elicits "meaning"; it becomes a conscious visual experience. The now human animal sees because it knows. As language saturates the environment, it creates the world of which we are conscious, which is never more extensive than that which language at any particular point of development is capable of creating. In accord with such a hypothesis, language becomes the *cause* and the sustaining content of consciousness. I will refer to this hereafter as "the causal hypothesis."

What must first be emphasized is that Heidegger and Burke would find this hypothesis abhorrent, both because of its pretension to exhaustively explanatory power and because of its reliance upon causation. The avoidance of the positivistic concept of cause is a law of Heidegger's thought and accounts in part for the difficulty of his texts. Heidegger and Burke would reject the assumptions and approach of this hypothesis and the ontological status of language that it suggests, but I can find no more effective way of expressing the magnitude of language as they conceive it. If their conceptions of language were translated into positivistic terms, the result would be something close to this hypothesis.

The causal hypothesis has its wholly reliable corollary in the later Heidegger's phenomenological treatment of the role of language. It is not clear that the corollary maintains in the early Heidegger. In *Being and Time*, what is called "discourse" may be understood as accounting for a prelinguistic articulation which is then communicated by language; language thus becomes only a "tool."[4] If this is a satisfactory understanding of language in *Being and Time*—and it may at least be questioned—it is nevertheless true that in the later work, as Joseph P. Fell says, "Heidegger's thinking moves from what might be called a prelinguistic ground to a linguistic ground."[5] In the later work language is "the lighting-concealing advent of Being itself."[6] "It is in words and language that things first come into being and are."[7] Heidegger's conception of language in the later work coincides very closely with the causal hypothesis. We must remember, however, that for Heidegger the relationship between language and Being is not causation but "equiprimordality." Nevertheless, the causal hypothesis can serve as a great consolation to the positivistically minded reader struggling with Heidegger's text for the first time.

In the case of Burke, as in that of Heidegger, the question of the causal hypothesis though revealing is in a sense inappropriate. The hypothesis violates a principle of Burke's thought which brings him into close harmony with phenomenological restraints. In his earliest theoretical work Burke articulates this principle: "We advocate nothing, then, but a return to inconclusiveness."[8] The alternatives to "inconclusiveness" are causal thinking and metaphysical thinking, or what Burke sometimes calls "going to the end of the line."[9] This tendency accounts for a person's being "rotten with perfection." Burke explains: "A given terminology contains various *implications*, and there is a corresponding 'perfectionist' tendency for men to attempt carrying out those implications." This is at work in all branches of knowledge, which end up with varied and conflicting determinisms: "there is a kind of 'terministic compulsion' to carry out the implications of one's terminology."[10] The causal hypothesis goes to the end of the line. It is a fundamental characteristic of Burke's thought that he never does. Burke's conception of language, and its approximation to the causal hypothesis, can be best understood in the light of his general project.

Burke's understanding coincides with that of Ernst Cassirer for whom "the Philosophy of Symbolic Forms in general inquires not into the empirical source of consciousness, but into its pure content."[11]

There is, however, little overlap between the work of Burke and Cassirer, except in Cassirer's single chapter entitled "Toward a Pathology of Symbolic Consciousness."[12] Cassirer's purpose is to trace three phases of development culminating in the pure symbolism of science and mathematics and to establish the continuity between these phases. These phases are "the sphere of expression" (mythic thought), that of "representation" (linguistic thought), and "the world of pure meaning" (science and mathematics).[13] Cassirer is concerned with the transitions between these phases and their essential unity; Burke is concerned with the way in which symbolism functions within the realms of "expression" and "representation" to create the human world.

It is true, nevertheless, that Burke's most fundamental argument can be stated in Cassirer's terms: "the intellectual impulse" which is a function of language "forever drives the human spirit beyond the sphere of what is immediately perceived and desired." And language creates "the distance separating the organic world and the world of human culture, the sphere of life and the sphere of the objective spirit."[14] Burke, to be sure, would avoid the overtones here of German idealism. He says,

> Once words are added (with the word-using faculty that a more honorific terminology would call "reason"), the purely biologic nature of pleasure, pain, love, hate, fear is quite transcended, since all are perceived through the coloration that the inveterate human involvement with words imports to them. . . . From that point on, no matter what man's motives might be in their nature as sheerly animal, they take on a wholly new aspect, as defined by the resources and embarrassments of their symbolism.[15]

In 1935 Burke formulated his theory of human culture as the product of language. Above the level of nature, language creates the distinctively human world; in this world language is the vehicle of freedom, and it achieves freedom by the generation of *purpose*. The argument leading to this conclusion Burke calls a "Metabiology." The concept of purpose when applied to human beings *"transcends biology in the strict sense of the term, in that men's social motives are not mere 'projections' of their nature as animal organisms not typically given to the motives of the verbal, or the symbolic."* Human freedom is not complete, not perfect. It is by no means the radical freedom of Jean-Paul Sartre, but the human realm is invested pervasively by alternatives which are the product of language. Man is capable of preference: "Man lives by purpose—and purpose is basically *preference*." [16] The possibility of preference generated by language distinguishes human beings fundamentally from animals. Things and animals *move;* human beings *act*. [17] The idea of action becomes pivotal for Burke's thought, central to the formulation of his basic perspective: this consists in "the view of man as 'poet', the approach to human motives in terms of action (with the poetic or dramatic terminologies being prized as the paradigms of action, a term that leads happily into the realms of both ethical and poetic piety, or into the scientific, too, by reason of the fact that 'symbolic' acts are grounded in 'necessitous' ones)." [18] Thus Burke formulates his basic position, called "Dramatism," which will culminate in his proposal of a philosophy of Being. Burke's "Dramatism" anticipated the theory of action, and emphasis on linguistic action as paradigmatic action, that has been central to recent Anglo-American philosophy.

Over and again Burke asserts the saturation of culture by, and its dependence upon, language: "Motives are distinctly linguistic products."—"For however the world is made, that's how language is made."—"Man *qua* man, is a symbol user. In this respect, every aspect of his 'reality' is likely to be seen through a fog of symbols."— "So far as sheerly empirical development is concerned it might be more accurate to say that language and the negative [which for Burke is crucial to language] 'invented' man."—Burke observes "how fantastically much of our 'Reality' could not exist for us, were it not for our profound and inveterate involvement in symbol systems." [19] Burke is as wary of the word "consciousness" as is Heidegger and like Heidegger he abjures causal thinking. Nevertheless, his emphasis upon the pervasiveness of language would seem to stop little short of the magnitude implicit in the causal hypothesis, and at one point he observes a correlate of the hypothesis with tacit approval. This occurs in reference to T. S. Eliot's doctoral dissertation, *Knowledge and Experience in the Philosophy of F. H. Bradley*. Burke quotes from the dissertation: "'Without words, no objects', he asseverates." Then there is a quotation of unusual length in a Burke text:

In any knowledge prior to speech the object is not so much an identity recognized as much as it is a similar way of acting; the identity is rather lived out than known. What we are here con-

cerned with is the explicit recognition of an object as such, and
I do not believe that this occurs without the beginnings of
speech. . . . Our only way of showing that we are attending to an
object is to show that it and ourself are independent entities,
and to do this we must have names. . . . We have no objects
without language.[20]

Burke expresses surprise and disappointment that Eliot does not
develop the argument further. We may observe that insofar as language is the cause of consciousness, it is difficult to distinguish Burke's
enterprise from that of phenomenology. Cassirer says, "Language . . .
reveals a noteworthy indifference toward the division of the world into
two distinct spheres, into an 'outward' and an 'inward' reality; so
much so, indeed, that this indifference seems inherent in its nature."
Burke conceives culture and consciousness (which are perhaps the
same) as saturated by language, and develops very clearly the rigorous
implications of this in a crucial essay entitled "Terministic Screens."
Every field of inquiry, every specialization, every theory, ideology,
philosophy, metaphysics, and every point of view is constituted by a
set of terms which is a terministic screen. Terministic screens are
what Wittgenstein in the *Tractatus* calls "networks," which, integrated
with "forms of life" in *Philosophical Investigations*, become "language
games." Any terminology, says Burke, "necessarily directs the attention into some channels rather than others." And, "even if any given
terminology is a *reflection* of reality, by its very nature as a terminology
it must be a *selection* of reality; and to this extent it must function also
as a *deflection* of reality." The correspondence is direct with Heidegger's fundamental point that language is both an unconcealment and a
concealment of Being: "Language is the lighting-concealing advent of
Being itself." We are never free of terministic screens. Terministic
screens constitute the category that Heidegger characterizes as "*a
fore-having, a fore-sight, and a fore-conception*," which is the basis of
all knowing and all perceiving. Burke arrives, then, at Heidegger's
hermeneutic circle which "is the expression of the existential *fore-
structure* of Dasein itself."[21] (The term "Dasein" will be explained
later in this study; for the present and tentatively we may take it to
mean "consciousness.") Even Burke's "Dramatism," he acknowledges, is a terministic screen.[22] Similarly for Heidegger "the phenomenology of Dasein is a *hermeneutic*."[23] Burke maintains that even
our senses interpret and that modes of personality and even psycho-

logical regression are factors of interpretation.[24] Every motive, says Burke, "is a term of interpretation."[25] Beyond what we can know only on the basis of terministic screens, there lies only "the abyss." Things, says Burke, "are the signs of words." Heidegger says that "there are no bare facts," and that is what Burke means when he says that the "semantic ideal is a fraud."[26]

Hermeneutics—in the form implicit in Nietzsche and explicit in Heidegger, which assumes the inevitability of interpretation—is essential to the conception of history shared by Burke and Heidegger. Burke has been criticized for underestimating history. The fact is simply that he, like Heidegger, has rejected historicism and for reasons closely related to those of Heidegger. For both writers history is fundamental, but historicism is an error: there is no present that is a simple product of the past. "Dasein's Being," says Heidegger, "is characterized by historicality," but Dasein is not the product of that historicality; rather "historicality" results from a more primordial character of Dasein. Dasein "*exists historically and can so exist only because it is temporal in the very basis of its Being.*" Historicality, however, is the source of that "fore-having" which makes interpretation inevitable, and as the result of which "the business of historiological interpretation is excluded *a priori* from the domain of rigorous knowledge" as measured by the values of the exact sciences.[27] Burke describes his position as "anhistoric," and it is so, he explains, because he has chosen a "philosophy of being" as the alternative to approaching "human problems *historically,* as in the philosophies of *becoming* which seem to have reached their flowering in Nineteenth Century thought (Goethe, Hegel, Marx, Darwin, Nietzsche, and the vast horde of lesser evolutionary and revolutionary thinkers)."[28] Burke emphatically asserts that a philosophy of being does not exclude the recognition of historical forces; rather the philosophy of historicism promotes submission to historical forces instead of encouraging their confrontation.[29] Similarly, Heidegger says that historicism "endeavors to alienate Dasein from its authentic historicality."[30] For both writers history offers possibilities from which we may choose, and history is a process in which our choices are a factor. Yet Being will be through and through historical.

With some idea of the necessary conceptions of language and history, we may now approach the question of a philosophy of Being—but slowly and at considerable distance. What is at issue in the concept of being was most acutely understood by Nietzsche, the apostle of "becoming," the nemesis of "being": "Happiness can be guaranteed only by being; change and happiness exclude one another." Substance, which we may take within the classical tradition as the equivalent of being, "cannot be sacrificed," says Nietzsche: "to let it go means: being no longer able to think." Nietzsche's destruction of being turns, in part, on a dichotomy that is defined by Cassirer as follows: "The world of metaphysics" is "governed by the concepts of substantiality and causality," and, as he makes clear, these concepts are in opposition. Cassirer says also, "Being . . . can only be understood as the counterpole and opposite of movement, its fixed, unchanging and immovable goal." Within the classical perspective, concepts align with "being" and "becoming" as follows—*being:* soul, substance, thing, category, entity, space, eternity; *becoming:* motion, change, relationship, cause, function, process, value (as involving relationship), time. For modern thought the problem of the concept of being has been described eloquently by Cassirer: "A progress from thing concepts to concepts of relation, from the positing of constant thing unities to that of pure lawful constance, is characteristic of the whole scientific view of the world in modern times beginning with Galileo and Kepler" and "this universal logical tendency was clearly at work in the system of classical [Newtonian] mechanics." Einstein's special theory of relativity, says Cassirer, brought this process to completion: "Here the substantial is completely transposed into the functional."[31]

How, then, may a modern thinker arrive at a philosophy of being? "Being certainly cannot be 'explained' in terms of entities," says Heidegger. Burke came to realize that a philosophy of being could not be constructed by "merely dismissing, by snobbery and legislative fiat, all the enlightenment that process-thinking has brought with it." Perhaps one might arrive, Burke thought, at "something like 'process-categories',", and we may take that term as a key.[32] Modern philosophies of being will have a kinship with relativity theory; as in Ezra Pound's conception of the symbol as "vortex," there will be a confluence of spatial and temporal elements.[33] A modern philosophy of being will be a *structure of becoming.* However, such is the case of all philosophies of being from the Middle Ages onward and, according to Heidegger, for the pre-Socratics as well. In scholastic philosophy act could be substance because it occurred within a metaphysical structure corresponding to myth. The "space of myth proves to be structural," says Cassirer.[34] It occurred also in Spinoza, for whom substance was not things within the world, but the distinctly metaphysical structure called "the totality." In Hegel thought becomes being as the great, all-inclusive, circular structure that realizes itself in time and history.

Nietzsche too came finally to a structure of becoming. The "eternal recurrence" solved a basic problem for Nietzsche. It meant that his "becoming" did not ever finally *become.* This would have given "becoming" a goal, which would have established again the ideal, and this would have subverted all that Nietzsche had to say. But the eternal recurrence of the same is something more than that. One of Nietzsche's notes is: "In place of 'metaphysics' and religion, the theory of eternal recurrence." He explains eternal recurrence: "In infinite time, every possible combination would at some time or another be realized; more: it would be realized an infinite number of times." So "a circular movement of absolutely identical series is thus demonstrated," and "if becoming is a great ring, then everything is equally valuable, eternal, necessary." He says, as "high point of the meditation": "That *everything recurs* is the closest *approximation of a world of becoming to a world of being.*" [35]

While various objections may be made to the philosophies of being of the past mentioned above, it may be noted that when they are not superstitious (mythical) they are cosmological; that is to say, all of them, including those of Hegel and Nietzsche, resort to a speculation enclosing the processes of becoming within a cosmic structure that bestows being and meaning upon a whole. The distinction of the thought of Heidegger and Burke is that, first, they require a continuous and more integral conjunction of becoming and being (time and space, function and form, process and structure) and, second, and more importantly, they seek being within whatever unidentified whole or totality might conceivably exist; they look for being within the intimacy of experience.

With that in mind, and with a risk of distortion that may be corrected later, I will adumbrate an outline of the project of Heidegger and Burke. They approach the classical dichotomies in the form originating in German idealism, the dichotomy of subject and object (though they reject these terms) which leads inevitably to Nietzsche's nihilism. From this dichotomy they depart anew. They examine separately the being of the subject and the being of the object. In simpler terms, they attempt to describe the structure of the being of knowing, or of consciousness, or of what Heidegger calls Dasein; then they at-

tempt to describe the structure of the being of the "thing." They assume an initial, intuitive knowledge of being, which Heidegger calls
ontic knowledge. Their analysis produces knowledge which Heidegger
distinguishes from *ontic* as *ontological.* Eventually, initially or finally,
the dichotomy of subject and object must be overcome and this will be
involved in an effort, building upon the structure of the being of the
subject and of the object, to arrive at a larger conception that will authenticate the being of the subject and the being of the thing. The
effort to achieve this larger conception Heidegger calls "the thinking
of Being." The error of past metaphysics is that it has always identified "beings" with "Being." The difference, which for Heidegger
is fundamental, he calls "the ontological difference." Burke, like
Heidegger, looks for the larger authenticating conception, and with
this in mind, and for special emphasis in connection with Burke, I do
not hesitate to adopt the Heideggerian convention of capitalizing the
"B" of "Being" considered ontologically. For such adaptation, Heidegger provides authority: "Every philosophical—that is, thoughtful—
doctrine of man's essential nature is *in itself alone* a doctrine of the
Being of beings." And "as soon as I thoughtfully say 'man's nature', I
have already said relatedness to Being."[36]

Discussion of the philosophy of being in Burke and Heidegger can
be facilitated by using for its heuristic value the concept of the "life-
world" that became the focus of philosophical interest for the later
Husserl, from *Ideas II* onward. "The counterconcept of 'life-world',
says Gadamer, "is without doubt the 'world of science'."[37] Cassirer
says, "we must choose between the immanent contents of consciousness—between reality as it presents itself to immediate sensation, to
perception and intuition—and that other transcendent reality that
reaches beyond it, namely the being to which theory, the scientific
concept, leads us." The two realms, says Cassirer, are incompatible.
"The concept of the 'life-world'," says Gadamer, "is the antithesis of
all objectivism."[38] A passage in Heidegger parallels the formulation
by Cassirer:

Let us think of the sun. Every day it rises and sets for us. Only a
very few astronomers, physicists, philosophers—and even they
only on the basis of a specialized approach which may be more
or less widespread—experience this state of affairs otherwise,
namely as a motion of the earth around the sun. But the appearance in which sun and earth stand, e.g. the early morning land-

scape, the sea in the evening, the night, is an appearing. This appearance is not nothing. Nor is it untrue. Nor is it a mere appearance of conditions in nature which are really otherwise. This appearance is historical and it is history, discovered and grounded in poetry and myth and thus an essential area of our world.

Only the tired latecomers with their supercilious wit imagine that they can dispose of the historical power of appearance by declaring it to be "subjective," hence very dubious.[39]

And "Being means appearing," says Heidegger: "Appearing is the very essence of Being." Gadamer emphasizes the social element of the life-world: "It is clear that the life-world is always at the same time a communal world and involves the existence of other people as well. It is a personal world, and in the natural attitude the validity of this personal world is assumed." The life-world is implicit in phenomenology, as Gadamer maintains. He points out that the concept underlies Heidegger's crucial analysis of "world" in *Being and Time.* The concept is conspicuously necessary to the late Heidegger, as will become obvious shortly, especially in the concept of the "thing." According to Gadamer, the concept of the life-world has its origin in Husserl's discovery in his earliest work "that there exist no monolithic and dogmatic concepts of giveness at all."[40] In effect, the authenticity of the life-world emerges from the default of objectivity, which leaves the life-world as the only possible locus of reality. What must be appreciated is that the shift of the basis of reality involved here is benefic in effect but catastrophic in magnitude.

The term "life-world" can be useful in discussing the work of Heidegger and Burke only if we keep in mind that for both men the centrality of language means a crucial deepening and broadening of the life-world.[41] For both the world is the world created by language and there is in this sense no other world than the life-world. Heidegger does not use the term, first, because Dasein is already "Being in the world" and, second, because the term "life-world" can comprehend different kinds of things, and it is thus too general for Heidegger's purposes. Most particularly, the life-world would contain both authentic and inauthentic experience. Nevertheless, some version of the concept is constantly present in his work. Burke thematizes the concept only in his repeated insistence on the reality of experience that results from language, the product of nothing less than the per-

vasive culture that constitutes man's "second nature." The life-world
is also implicit in his contrasting of the terminologies of Dramatism
with those of science.[42] With such reservations in mind, I will regu-
larly use the term "life-world" and distinguish it from the "theoretical
world" or theoretical or scientific knowledge. Not only is the concept
relevant. It will be possible later to argue that, despite Heidegger's re-
jections of various solipsisms of others, we may find in both Heidegger and Burke an ontological authorization of the life-world based on
a kind of solipsism of language. Both men would reject the term "solipsism," but it is significant that Max Scheler, Heidegger's close
friend, criticized him for the solipsism in which his thought began.[43]

While it is Nietzsche who poses Heidegger's problem, his method
stems from his teacher Edmund Husserl, whom he succeeded in the
chair of philosophy at the University of Freiburg. The question of
Being, says Heidegger, "is one which must be treated phenomenologically."[44] A brief indication of Husserl's method will be helpful in a
number of ways.

Phenomenology was the study of "subjectivity," the study of consciousness, and—as consciousness was always "intentional," always
consciousness of something—the study of things as they present
themselves to consciousness. The cry of phenomenology was "back to
the things themselves," though it is doubtful that Husserl ever got
back to "the things themselves." Before phenomenological investigation could begin, it was necessary that consciousness be "reduced" to
its primordial state. The reduction, as described in *Ideas I*, required
that one exclude, or "bracket," all knowledge derived from objective
science and, more than that, all knowledge of objectivity, all knowledge of anything, including one's body, as having existence external to
consciousness.[45] Consciousness was thus reduced to its condition of
"transcendental subjectivity." In one further step, called the "eidetic
reduction," consciousness was brought into a primordial purity of the
"intuition of essence." With this reduction, one arrived at the realm
of "transcendental idealism," and there phenomenology would begin
the "endless tasks" of its investigations.

What Husserl's phenomenology investigates, the knowledge with
which it begins, is the *appearances* experienced in reduced consciousness. What is experienced here is not things as they exist in themselves externally to consciousness but *representations* of things. Husserl's
thought is thus continuous with what Heidegger rejects as "representative thinking." Representative thinking posed for Husserl from the

outset a perhaps insuperable problem. "Phenomenology," says Paul Ricoeur, "was born under the menace of a true solipsism."[46] Husserl contended that the solipsism of his reduction could be escaped, objectivity could be reestablished, by a logic that proceeded from the bracketed condition achieved in the eidetic reduction, the realm of certainty (the realm of certainty, because there can be no doubt that we are experiencing *something*). This logical procedure, which Husserl undertook most notably in the "Fifth" of the *Cartesian Meditations*, would solve the problem of the existence of a world external to consciousness which Descartes had solved only by the assumption of a God who would not deceive us.[47] With this link firmly established, phenomenology, beginning in certainty and incorporating the external world with this certainty, would become "rigorous science." Husserl's solution of the problem of solipsism is, at best, open to doubt, and, lacking a solution of the problem, Husserlian phenomenology remains irredeemably isolated, incapable of connection with any other body of knowledge.

Heidegger's phenomenology is a radical departure from Husserl. It is essential to Heidegger that he rejected the subjectivity of Husserl's transcendental reduction and the idealism of his eidetic reduction. Heidegger confronts the question of solipsism bluntly, declaring that the problem, which Kant called "the scandal of philosophy," is no scandal because there is no problem.[48] The problem arose for Husserl only because he continued the error which invalidates Western philosophy after the pre-Socratics, the error of "representative thinking," in which experience is not of things but of "representations" of things. Thus all past philosophy remains the victim of "subjectivity" and is what Heidegger calls "metaphysics." Representative thinking and subjectivity are errors, Heidegger maintains, because there is no such thing as the thing-in-itself external to consciousness. There is and can be no knowledge of anything that is not mediated. The world as we experience it—the world as it appears—is the only world there is: it is the primordial world in relation to which science and theoretical explanation are derivative. This position, which is fundamental to all Heidegger's thought, is presented most clearly in a brief passage of *Being and Time:*

What we 'first' hear is never noises or complexes of sounds but the creaking wagon, the motor-cycle. We hear the column on the march, the north wind, the woodpecker tapping, the fire crackling.

It requires a very artificial and complicated frame of mind to 'hear' a 'pure noise'.[49]

What this means is that we may make no distinction between the content of consciousness and what Heidegger calls the "world," which is the context of all possible experience, the "world" comprised as a totality of relationships. With this in mind we are in a position to understand the key term of Heidegger's thought. That term is *Dasein,* which is usually translated as "There-being" or "Being-there," though late in his life Heidegger expressed the preference that the *Da* of *Dasein* be translated as "openness."[50] I will not translate the term, following the practice of the translators of *Being and Time.* The meaning of the term derives from a distinction that Husserl made between the function and the structure of consciousness, on one hand, and its contents on the other, which he called respectively *noesis* and *noema.*[51] We may say first that in the word "Dasein" Heidegger refers to the function and structure of consciousness. We could say that Dasein is consciousness if we could say that it is the "world," for the content of consciousness and the "world" cannot be separated. Their descriptions are one and the same description. In a sense Dasein is both: "Dasein *is* its world existingly." This is what is meant when Heidegger indicates the first characteristic of Dasein: "'Dasein' means Being-in-the-world." Heidegger says,

The fact that motor-cycles and waggons are what we proximally hear is the phenomenal evidence that in every case Dasein, as Being-in-the-world, already dwells *alongside* what is ready-to-hand within-the-world; it certainly does not dwell proximally alongside 'sensations'.[52]

This radical position is fundamental to understanding Heidegger, and the struggle to maintain it accounts for part of the difficulty of the text of *Being and Time.* The position is expressed by the later Heidegger as follows: "With all our correct representations we would get nowhere, we could not even presuppose that there already is manifest something to which we can conform ourselves, unless the unconcealedness of beings had already exposed us to, placed us in, that lighted realm in which every being stands for us and from which it withdraws." Heidegger tells us that "Dasein hears because it understands," and, with the reservation previously noted concerning language in the early Heidegger, we may say that it is only in and by virtue of language that Dasein understands.[53] It would seem clear that Heidegger can overcome Husserl's kind of solipsism because of the decisive role Heidegger allots to language.

I will now take up Heidegger's thinking of the Being of Dasein. Any effort to deal with Heidegger briefly must be tainted by a tendency to translate his thought back into the Western "metaphysics" that it was his purpose to escape.[54] At best such an effort will fail to suggest the rigor and complexity of Heidegger's thought. However, the structures I will report are the structures in the description of which his thought culminates. My purpose is to demonstrate homologies between the thought of Heidegger and that of Burke, and in this the minimal demand for exposition of Heidegger is to assure that Burke and Heidegger are not equated.

In becoming there is no *present,* only *past* and *future.* For Heidegger presence (being) requires a present, not in the "everyday" realm of clock time, but in time as phenomenologically observed, and this involves his most subtle and difficult phenomenological operation. The dominant orientation of Dasein is to the future: Dasein is always "ahead-of-itself," but what it projects into the future has its origin in the past, and in the confluence of future and past there is engendered the present. Heidegger's more difficult statement is as follows: "The character of 'having been' arises from the future, and in such a way that the future which 'has been' (or better, which 'is in the process of having been') releases from itself the Present." This is the central formulation of *Being and Time.* It is the meaning of Heidegger's famous conclusion that time is "the horizon of Being."[55] Gadamer interprets this to mean that Being *is* time.[56] This conception is enforced by an effort by Heidegger in *Being and Time* to derive space from time.[57] Heidegger will later conclude this effort to be a mistake and he will abandon the conception of time as "the horizon of Being" as the basis for thinking Being. In *Being and Time,* however, Heidegger's conception of the relationship of present to past and future is the basis on which he attempts to think the Being of Dasein. The conception is inherent in the hermeneutic position, and any effort to derive a conception of time from the thought of Burke produces a configuration closely similar to Heidegger's. Lentricchia says, "The 'present' that

Burke defines is nothing but the intersection of past and future." [58] In Heidegger, as in Burke, this structure of the temporality of Dasein emerges in the experience of Dasein in larger dimensions than have been suggested here, and these larger dimensions, including especially the historical dimension, must now be outlined.

The most comprehensive way of sketching out Heidegger's development of the Being of Dasein, which is the burden of *Being and Time,* is to begin with Heidegger's conception of the "they-world." It is the world of "everydayness," in which all of us find ourselves "proximally and for the most part," to use Heidegger's constant qualifier. The they-world is the inconstant world of "affairs," of distraction and fragmentation. It is characterized by "idle talk, curiosity and ambiguity," for it is the "public" world in which the "'they' prescribes one's state-of-mind and determines what and how one 'sees'." In the they-world, idle talk is discourse that "has lost its primary relationship-of-Being towards the entity talked about" and "communicates rather by following the route of *gossiping* and *passing the word along.*" The they-world is "lost in the making present of the 'today'" and "it understands the 'past' in terms of the 'present'," thus violating the basic structure of the temporality of Dasein.[59] This is the error of "historicism," which "endeavours to alienate Dasein from its authentic historicality." The they-world is rootless: "In awaiting the next new thing, it has already forgotten the old." And in this, "the 'they' evades choice," for choices have their source in the past. Dasein's "absorption in Being-with-one-another" Heidegger calls "fallenness." Dasein has "fallen away . . . from itself as an authentic potentiality for Being its Self, and has fallen into the 'world'." This absorption has "the character of Being-lost in the publicness of the 'they'."[60] Falling defines the "'inauthenticity' of Dasein." The they-world is a world of "not-Being."[61]

The possibility of Dasein's withdrawing itself from the they-world exists because Dasein, however "fallen" and "lost" (both of which are not moral but technical terms), is never without some kind of obscured and distorted knowledge of Being, "the preontological understanding of Being." This point, which is a constant theme of *Being and Time,* is fundamental in that it provides the basic authentication of the project of "the thinking of Being." Heidegger says, "In falling, Dasein *itself . . .* is something from which it has already fallen away," and that "something" is the possibility of the Being of Dasein.[62] A kind of knowledge of Being is implicit in the phenomena which Heidegger calls "care" (*Sorge*), "anxiety" (*Angst*), "conscience," and "guilt." (Conscience and guilt are not concerned with expressions of moral failure, but underlie its possibility, as anxiety underlies the possibility of fear.) Care is a constant, essentially identifiable with the structure of the temporality of Dasein.[63] So care is "Dasein's Being."[64] Care gives rise to "uncanniness," and uncanniness is a sense of being "not-at-home."[65] Uncanniness is "the most elemental way in which thrown Dasein is disclosed" and "it puts Dasein's Being-in-the-world face to face with the 'nothing' of the world." Dasein, or care, knows itself as "the null basis for its null projection" in the lostness of the "they" and is thus guilty. There is a call of conscience in which "Dasein calls itself." Thus anxiety makes manifest in Dasein its "freedom of choosing itself and taking hold of itself." Anxiety "individualizes." This individualization "brings Dasein back from its falling, and makes manifest to it that authenticity and inauthenticity are possibilities of its Being." The call of conscience "reaches who wants to be brought back."[66] It establishes a possibility of choosing.

We must consider now the possibility for the authentic Being which Dasein can choose. There is something about Dasein that is incomplete. The "primary item in care is the 'ahead-of-itself'." This means that "there is always something *still outstanding*," there is "*constantly something still to be settled.*"[67] Dasein is "Being-in-the-world and it is "care," and it is also "thrownness." That is, it has been "delivered over" to the beings only in relation to which it can have its Being, and the term suggests the adventitiousness, the randomness, of the fact that Dasein finds itself "alongside" one particular set of beings rather than another.[68] But thrownness also means that Dasein is on its own: it has been "released . . . to itself." As "delivered over to itself," Dasein "is the possibility of Being free *for* its ownmost potentiality-for-Being," that is, a potentiality for Being which is not "relational," does not depend upon its relationship to other beings, a possibility for Being which is peculiarly its own, "the possibility of the measureless impossibility of existence." Dasein's "ownmost-possibility-for-Being" is death. Death "belongs in a distinctive sense to the Being of Dasein." Death, however, is not something we can know: there is no way of "'picturing' to oneself the actuality which is possible, and so forgetting its possibility." Heidegger says, "a psychology of 'dying' gives information about the 'living' of the person who is 'dying', rather than about dying itself."[69] It is thus necessary to interpret death as "Being-towards-the-end," which is an aspect of "Dasein's basic state."[70] Dasein, which is "Being-in-the-world" and "care" and "thrownness," is also "Being-towards-the-end." Anxiety "amounts to the disclosedness of the fact that Dasein exists as thrown Being towards its end," and it is chiefly thus that thrownness is revealed to us. "With death," says Heidegger, "Dasein stands before itself in its ownmost potentiality-for-Being." Generally, however, Dasein attempts to obscure and evade death; it maintains itself "in an inauthentic Being-towards-death." In this evasion Dasein is abetted by the "they," which "does not permit us the courage for anxiety in the face of death." In the they-world we experience "temptation, tranquillization and alienation" which are the marks of "falling"; falling, or "everyday Being-towards-death," is "a constant *fleeing in the face of death.*" [71] In the they-world and in the evasion of Being-towards-death, Dasein eludes its Self and exists inauthentically.

But anxiety reveals the possibility of freedom and authenticity. Because Dasein *is* its possibilities, "it *can,* in its very Being, 'choose' itself and win itself." This choosing of itself it achieves when, ceasing to evade its death, in anticipation it affirms its death. This affirmation is a "choosing," which is called "*resoluteness.*" It is "only in the antici-pation of death that resoluteness as Dasein's *authentic* truth has reached the *authentic certainty* which *belongs* to it." One "becomes free for one's own death, one is liberated from one's lostness in those possibilities which may accidentally thrust themselves upon one," and anticipatory resoluteness "shatters all one's tenaciousness to whatever existence one has reached." In resoluteness Dasein "stands before itself," and "all its relations to any other Dasein have been undone"; it "has been wrenched away from the 'they'." [72] Death "individualizes"; resolute-ness "includes the possibility of existing as a *whole potentiality for Being.*" Being "free *for* one's own death," Dasein is also "free for its ownmost possibilities," which are "understood as finite." Finitude, which for Heidegger means both mortality and the limitation of knowledge, unquestionably underlies the attitude of piety that in-forms Heidegger's work, especially the later work. Resoluteness and openness to anxiety, rather than a fleeing from it, bring strength—and something else: "Along with the sober anxiety which brings us face to face with our individualized potentiality-for-Being, there goes an unshakable joy in this possibility." [73]

Resoluteness does not result in withdrawing into isolation; rather it results in a new integrity in human relations: "Only by authentically Being-their-Selves in resoluteness can people authentically be with one another." It is of crucial importance that resoluteness alters the meaning of history, a meaning which becomes authentic. The present is no longer lost in the they-world but can achieve its primordial character as a fold of future and past, and history becomes a past from which one can choose for the future: "When historicality is authentic, it understands history as the 'recurrence' of the possible, and knows that a possibility will recur only if existence is open for it fatefully, in a moment of vision, in resolute repetition." Dasein is now capable of "handing down to itself the possibility it has inherited." The moment of vision is the moment of vision "for 'its time'." Hence, with resoluteness the essential structure of the temporality of Dasein structures history: "In resoluteness, the Present is not only brought back from distraction with objects of one's closest concern, but it gets held in the future and in having been," and it is such a Present that becomes the "*moment of vision.*" [74] Resoluteness brings Dasein to its Being and is the condition for the "thinking of Being."

We may note that in the themes of *Being and Time* that have now been summarized there is a great deal of Nietzsche. In the repetition of possibility there is a transformed echo of the eternal recurrence, and in being open to possibilities "fatefully" there is a suggestion of Nietzsche's "men who are destinies." [75] In Fragment 569 of *The Will to Power* Nietzsche contemplates the ontological primacy of the "thing" and the life-world. [76] Of death Nietzsche says, "One must convert the stupid physiological fact into a moral necessity. So to live that one can also *will at the right time to die.*" And resoluteness is not very different from the *amor fati* of Nietzsche's "Dionysian affirmation of the world as it is." [77]

Being and Time is in one sense a propaedeutic to the thinking of Being. The work develops the Being of Dasein, which is "something like 'Being'." "Being has been disclosed in a preliminary way, though non-conceptually." [78] The thinking of Being would involve thinking also the Being of the world and of "things" in the world, and that was to have been the purpose of a proposed second part of the work which was never written. The consummation of the thinking of Being remained the burden of Heidegger's thought all his life, and it is in the later Heidegger that we find the thinking of the Being of the thing, to which we will return hereafter. Other aspects of *Being and Time* will be taken up as we proceed.

chapter 3

Burke's Act and Paradox of Being

BURKE's second theoretical work, and his most important in the sense that it is seminal of all those that follow, is entitled *Permanence and Change.*[1] The correspondence with the title *Being and Time* reflects both an essential correspondence of interest while reflecting also the diversity of approaches: on the one hand practical—psychological and social—on the other, metaphysical, though Burke fully understood that his position, too, was ultimately metaphysical. Nevertheless, in a section of *Permanence and Change* entitled "Toward a Philosophy of Being," Burke seemed chiefly interested in method, in the kind of approach that would guide his discussion of "man in general." From the first Burke understood "terministic screens," and one screen could be more fruitful than another. So he would "return through *symbolism* [my italics] to a philosophy of *being* [Burke's italics]." Spinoza's "concern with man *sub specie aeternitatis*" will have its corollary in "the *metaphor* [my italics] of a *norm* [Burke's italics], the notion that at bottom the aims and genius of man have remained fundamentally the same, that temporal events may cause him to stray far from his Sources but that he repeatedly struggles to restore, under new particularities, the same basic pattern of the 'good life'."[2] Burke sees the concept of being as essential to understanding the realm of human culture and to the conduct of human intercourse: "Human relationships must be *substantial,* related by the copulative, the 'is' of 'being'." It follows that there can be no "'science of human relations':" for "there is a strategic or crucial respect in which this is impossible: namely: there can be no 'science' of substance."[3] Similarly, Gadamer, Heidegger's wholly faithful disciple, argues that "the methodological ideal of rational construction that dominates modern mathematically based science" is inadequate to human relations and that only in "what exists, what man recognizes as existent and significant" can the "process of understanding practiced in the moral sciences recognize itself." There is no question, however, that Burke sees the question of being as involving more than an intellectual tool, and more, indeed, than a terministic screen. Like Nietzsche, he sees himself as a "propounder of new meanings," and in the final paragraph of *Permanence and Change* we find him conceiving the thinking of being as does Heidegger: it is a means of escaping from the "they-world." It is, says Burke, a perspective "for dwarfing of our impatience. We in the cities rightly grow shrewd at appraising man-made institutions—but beyond these tidy concentrations of rhetoric and traffic, there lies the eternally unsolvable Enigma, the preposterous fact that both existence and nothingness are equally unthinkable."[4]

In Burke's thought, "act" is the central idea first and last; it is the focus of the structure of becoming which is the culmination of the development of Burke's system, which he usually calls "Dramatism," but sometimes "Logology." Act is made possible by language, which creates choices, requiring preferences, which are purposes. Language creates alternatives and it also sometimes creates the means of choosing between them. Burke's most impressive demonstration of this argument is presented in the astonishing work called *The Rhetoric of Religion: Studies in Logology.*[5] In the study entitled "The First Three Chapters of Genesis" Burke demonstrates that not only these chapters but the entire Hebraic-Christian myth can be derived dialectically ("logologically") from the concept of "Ordinance."[6] In "Verbal Action in St. Augustine's Confessions" Burke concentrates on the moment of conversion when Augustine, consenting to the idea of the Father and the Son, balked at the idea of the Holy Ghost, or Love, and stood suspended between the attractions of his mistresses, his "toys," and the lure of Christianity, the linguistically created alternative. The pivotal fact lay in Augustine's having been much impressed by the Manicheans' "'show of continence'": "*Continentia* is a highly important word in Augustine's scheme. Grammatically feminine, at the critical point," says Burke, "it becomes personified." Burke points to the passage which, "beginning with a reference to his mistresses ('toys of toys, vanities of vanities'), turns into a paean to 'continency' personified as a 'fecund mother of children and joys', who has God as her husband." Burke sees in this the necessary transformation leading to the actual conversion, narrated in the succeeding chapter of the *Confessions*. The problem of Love, the Holy Spirit, was solved when "the general lure of corporeal *mistresses* could be replaced by the single, spiritual, dignified maternal figure of Continentia," and Burke repeats, "who had God as her husband."[7] Burke treats the conversion within the context of theological controversy in which Augustine was immersed, but he sees psychological transformation made possible by the symbolic resources of language as the fundamental occurrence in the process of the conversion. Clearly, Freud is a massive presence here, but even so brief a report of Burke's discussion is sufficient to suggest Burke's basic revision of Freud, which consists largely in the conception of language as providing the patterns in which psychological dynamisms function, Burke thus anticipating Jacques Lacan, whose work is based chiefly on this discovery.[8] Lacan denies that this conception is a revision of Freud, but few will be convinced on this point.

For Burke, however, the act is more than some combination of verbal and libidinal determinisms: "Every act is a miracle." It is a "synthesis" of an "infinity of components." Gadamer's formulation is essentially the same: "Every act, as an element of life, remains connected with the infinity of life that manifests itself in it." Hence it is for Burke that "most of our significant concerns with basic cultural matters lie in a territory where working models cannot possibly be made" and the philosophical claims of science "come close to downright hypocrisy." The act has another essential characteristic; it brings something new into the world: "For an act can be an act only if it is *free* (if it is not free, it is but compulsive motion); and it can be free only insofar as it has novelty, in adding something to the previous total of necessary conditions." The conceptions of the act as novelty and as synthesis of an infinity of components are thoroughly harmonious. Though Burke does not systematize on this point—in abhorrence of system and in abjuring both mysticism, and, insofar as possible, metaphysics—his thought in its great diversity is rigorously consistent, and the logic here is quite clear: an infinity of components may be referred to, but by definition it lies beyond the finitude of knowledge and experience; the act brings something from beyond the realm of knowledge into experience. Here we are but a step away from Heidegger's conception of truth as the "unconcealment" of Being. For Burke there is a *sense* in which "the 'creating of something out of nothing' might be called the very essence of an *act*." So "God's creative fiat . . . is the paradigm of all action" and "God thus becomes analyzable as the word for the idea of a wholly free act."[9]

As early as *Permanence and Change* (1935) Burke had fully developed the idea of the act.[10] In this work he also contemplated the possibility of unifying modern thought: "Out of all this overlapping, conflicting, and supplementing of interpretative frames, what arises as a totality?" And such a synthesis seemed necessary: "The myriad of orientations will be tragically wasted, the genius of one of the world's most vigorous centuries will be allowed to go unused, unless we can adapt its very welter of interpretations as skeptical grounding for our own certainties."[11] It would seem clear that if the "welter of interpretations" were to become "skeptical grounding for our own certainties," then the interpretations would not be rejected or ignored, but they would be denied their claim to autonomy; they would, in short, be recognized as relegated to the limitations, the finitude, of human knowledge. For that, indeed, a system would be required, within which knowledge could be subordinated. Burke had not yet discovered the relationship of the idea of the act to all this, but we may develop the pending question. Acts are never complete, never totally free.[12] But insofar as they are acts and are free, they, in the infinity of their components, are unknowable, unanalyzable. What would be the relationship of act to the welter of interpretations? The answer that came in *A Grammar of Motives* (1945) was that the act is the unknowable center of human knowledge, which thus assumes the status of its finitude.

A Grammar of Motives is built upon two concepts—first, the concept of the act; second, and closely related to act, Burke's version of the concept of *substance*. The problems posed for Burke by the concept of act are illuminated by his conception of the role of language. Only in one concept does Burke's systematic thought conceive of a principle that breaks free of language: it is in the concept of the act. Indeed, language creates the alternatives that require the choice that is the act. At times, as in the analysis of Augustine's conversion, language may be seen as facilitating the act, but if it explained or caused the act, if it did the choosing, then Burke would find himself not only in linguistic solipsism but committed to a linguistic determinism as well. Obviously language cannot provide the motive force of the act, which is by definition free. There must be something beyond language that is free to act. Where outside of language is to be found the origin of act? If with the concept of act one breaks out of the realm of language, at what does he arrive? Certainly not for Burke at materialistic explanation.

This problem Burke faced squarely when he acknowledged that the concepts of "act" and "motivation" are incompatible: "strictly speaking, the act of an agent would be the movement not of one *moved* but of a *mover* (a mover of the self or of something else by the self). For an act is by definition active, whereas to be moved (or motivated) is by definition passive."[13] In other words, to *explain* act would be to ascribe a motivation, or cause, of act, by which it would cease to be an act. On the other hand, simply to accept the unexplainable would be to open oneself to the charge of mysticism, or such would have been especially a danger in 1945. Nevertheless, the real import of what Burke is saying here is that act is not to be explained, and to see in "the motivation of an act" the "paradox of substance," as Burke does here, is not to explain act. Clearly, the concept of act posed a difficulty for Burke, and Lentricchia goes so far as to see in the passage under consideration a deconstruction of "act" and of "the subject-agent."[14] Such a reading is entirely admissible, providing that we read into Burke the full force of deconstructionist intention. For Burke "deconstruction" here would mean only, and necessarily, that act remains unexplainable, and the elimination of metaphysical, that is, unexplained, concepts from his thought is quite contrary to Burke's intention. The deconstruction of the "subject," though not the "agent," Burke has achieved elsewhere and in a way that does not involve the concept of the act.[15] The concept of the act has remained central to Burke's thought throughout the forty years since *A Grammar of Motives*.

The problems created by the concept of act for Burke in 1945, when positivism was still in sway, are perhaps the reason why *A Grammar of Motives* seems sometimes marred by the traces of a struggle. The original manuscript, Burke tells us, ran to nearly 200,000 words, "of which the present book is a revision and abridgement." When Burke had first raised the question of arriving at "a totality," in 1935, he had found that all who had attempted that, including Bentham, Marx, Freud, Jung, and Bergson, had arrived "close to the edges of a mysticism as arrant as that of any 'disorganized' medieval seer." It seems highly probable that the temptations of mysticism, or the appearance of mysticism, were the burden of much that was omitted from the original manuscript, perhaps some 24,000 words, this having the nature of what Burke calls his "pre-pre-introductions." The omitted material must have struggled over the implications of the idea of the act. In the "pre-pre-introduction" that remains in the text, Burke not only acknowledges but insists upon the fact that "dialectical and metaphysical issues *necessarily* figure in the subject of motivation," the subject of motivation being the ultimate concern of all Burke's thought. His recourse for the moment, however, is to say that "to explain our position, we shall show how it can be applied."[16]

For present purposes the application can be considered briefly. From the concept of act, Burke arrives at his basic analytic tool, though it is much more than a tool. The derivation is as follows: "any complete statement of motives will offer *some kind* of answers to these five questions: what was done (act), when or where it was done (scene), who did it (agent), how he did it (agency), and why (purpose)." The result is Burke's "Pentad" of key terms: "Act, Scene, Agent, Agency, Purpose."[17] Burke points out that the terms correspond to Aristotle's causes, which are, of course, causes not of events but of being.[18] A major argument is that "seven primary philosophical languages" result from taking one or the other of the five terms of the pentad as basic.[19] This yields the following classification: realism (act), materialism (scene), idealism (agent), pragmatism (agency), mysticism (purpose). Nominalism and rationalism are derivative from these.[20] Burke's analysis is complex and extensive. Most arguments, says Burke, focus not in a single term of the pentad but in a "ratio" between the terms. The five terms allow for ten ratios, says Burke, but the scene-act and scene-agent ratios are most important; we find them everywhere.[21] The "ratios," Burke says, "are essentially analogies." That is, by a "'scene-act ratio' we mean that the nature of the act is implicit, or analogously present in the nature of the scene, etc." Ratios are also areas of ambiguity, and it is in such areas that dialectical transformations may occur: "At every point where the field covered by any one of these terms overlaps upon the field covered by any other, there is an alchemic opportunity, whereby we can put one philosophy or doctrine of motivation into the alembic, make the appropriate passes and take out another."[22] The pentad is thus "a generating principle" making it possible to "'anticipate'" the seven "primary philosophic languages."

One "may make his way continuously from any one of them to any of the others." [23] On the basis of dialectical transformations occurring within areas of ambiguity, such transformations govern the development of philosophy historically and the development of individual philosophies.

Burke demonstrates these principles in an extraordinarily wide range of thought, including that of Plato, Aristotle, Plotinus, Aquinas, Hobbes, Spinoza, Locke, Hume, Berkeley, Leibniz, Kant, Hegel, Darwin, Marx, James, Freud, Dewey, and Santayana. [24] What this amounts to—long before Derrida—is what might be called a "deconstruction" of philosophy in general and of most of the significant philosophers. The basic method, as in *The Rhetoric of Religion* and in an earlier "deconstruction" of Freud, is to demonstrate that concepts based on presumably more rigorous and objective arguments can be generated dialectically. [25] Burke's conception of language means that philosophy as it has been traditionally conceived is impossible. It means that despite "the occasional scientific pretenses of philosophers" their work must be conceived as "poetic action." [26] With that term a distinction is required. Burke's "deconstructions," unlike Derrida's, do not consign the concepts which are their objects to a scrap heap of history. The term "poetic action" can never in Burke's vocabulary imply total denigration.

If all philosophy has been "poetic action," we may then inquire concerning the philosophy that Burke himself is in the process of developing. Is this, too, poetic action? The answer is yes, but in a different way: Burke's philosophy is a description of poetic action. The pentad as the structure of the act is also the structure of the poetic act. Thus poetry is continuous with life, and in that alone the Kantian aesthetic is excluded. We will see that Heidegger's thought in its basic conceptions also excludes the Kantian aesthetic. The pentad, which is the structure of the poetic act and of all acts, is at the center of Burke's philosophy.

But then there is another question. Is not the pentad "the cold-blooded Platonism of the most extreme kind of structuralism" and therefore needing in its turn to be deconstructed, as Lentricchia implies? [27] The answer seems clearly to be: structuralism, yes, but of a very special kind. Obviously, the pentad is a structure, but in no sense can it be considered a "frozen" structure. It is a synchrony to which the diachrony of "act" is antecedent and a synchrony in which diachrony is implicit. If it is true, as Lentricchia maintains, that synchrony and diachrony are a "conflict of hermeneutical impulses" in Burke, then the conflict is effectively resolved in the pentad.[28] In the concept of the act, the pentad is open to history; history is implicit in it. It is, in fact, a description of the condition necessary to the conception of time that Lentricchia has so aptly found in Burke's thought, and this is a conception necessary to the conception of history which Burke shares with Heidegger. It is true, and remarkably so, that the pentad poses no less than a means of organizing human knowledge in a way comparable to the synthesis of knowledge that occurs continuously in Burke's thought; it provides, as Burke says, a scheme of placement.[29] But such a synthesis would not constitute a "totalization" of history; no possible similarity can be found with Hegel. The history which the pentad might synthesize is a history of which we would know neither the margins nor the beginning nor the end. In the pentad the past becomes simply the condition of a conjunction with the future. In Burke's thought there are no cosmological reaches, only, as we will see, some effort to make a local connection with an indeterminate enveloping scene.

What is at issue in such a structure as the pentad is the possibility of thinking; we cannot think without structures, as Nietzsche has assured us. Lentricchia's strictures against the pentad must be taken as an effort to avert the knee-jerk reaction against Burke of a mindless and derivative deconstructionism that can tolerate nothing but intellectual desolation, Nietzsche's wasteland. Lentricchia makes it clear that he knows that without structures we cannot even deconstruct, a point concerning which his comments on substance are eloquent.[30] Lentricchia is right in his eventual happy designation of Burke as a "critical structuralist," but Burke can have that character only if act is *not* deconstructed.[31] Unless act can be taken as having one of many originary roles in history, neither Burke's concept of history nor Heidegger's will hold up. Burke's own comparison of his structures with those of Kant have a point, but in the contemporary intellectual milieu that is misleading. When Burke spoke of being "concerned with the basic forms of thought," he would have averted posterity's alarm by saying "basic forms of thinking." What Burke has described is by no means a "disembodied geometry of mind."[32] The pentad places the act within its environment, confronting, accepting, and, in some measure, making history.

The position I maintain here is capable of some illumination by observing a dimension in which the pentad has a direct correlative in

Heidegger's early thought. To make this point I will undertake a formulation concerning the pentad that Burke does not make explicit. Indeed, though Burke tells us how to use the pentad, he never tells us explicitly what the pentad is a structure of. Nevertheless, we may say that on one hand the pentad describes consciousness *in its relation to* its environment. On the other hand, we may take the pentad to be the structure of consciousness *as it is registered* in the world that it creates, this structure being most apparent and of most obvious relevance for analysis in the paradigmatic act of human creation, the work of art. Burke's thought is continually loyal to the idea that "man," or consciousness, can be analyzed only as it expresses itself in the structure of the world which it creates, as it expresses itself in language. It follows that any effort to characterize the pentad finds its corollary in that characterization of Dasein whereby we could say that it is consciousness if we could also say that it is the "world."

Though Nietzsche exploded the concept of being and substance and considered the distinction between theoretical and practical (life-world) thought to be dangerous, he acknowledged the necessity of the life-world: "In order to think and infer it is necessary to assume beings. . . . Knowledge and becoming exclude one another." More impressed with this fact than Nietzsche, Burke, in *A Grammar of Motives*, refuses to relinquish the concept of substance. The traditional conception of substance, however, has been transformed; it has become the "paradox of substance." The paradox consists in this, that "to tell what a thing is, you place it in terms of something else." More emphatically, we must define a thing on the basis of its relationships, and "to define a thing in terms of its context, we must define it in terms of what it is not." [33] We may say of the opposing parts of this paradox that the life-world contributes substance, the reification implicit in language, and the world of theory contributes the dissolution of substance. The paradox arises because both worlds are affirmed. The life-world and the theoretical world must be sustained in inevitable tension.

The two aspects of things which Burke conceives as paradoxically joined in his conception of the thing, Heidegger treats in *Being and Time* as two separate and distinct modes of being called "ready-to-hand" and "present-at-hand." Things as they serve our purposes, things which exist for us as part of our affairs and intentions, Heidegger calls *das Zeug*, which is translated as "equipment." Equipment has the kind of being called "ready-to-hand." [34] But under different circumstances the same entity may have very different kinds of being. There are two meanings which may be intended when we say, "The hammer is heavy." We may mean that the hammer is too heavy for the task involved. In this case the hammer is "equipment"; it is ready-to-hand. Contrastingly, we may mean simply that the hammer has weight, or heaviness. The hammer has now the character of being "present-at-hand." It has lost its character as "equipment" and is being considered in itself. It has become an object; it is seen in the abstract perspective that characterizes science.[35] It has become an object of theoretical knowledge. Of special importance for Heidegger's later thinking of the Being of the thing is that the object, the "present-at-hand," no longer has a "place": "its place becomes a spatio-temporal position, a 'world-point', which is in no way distinguished from any other." In the next-to-last paragraph of *Being and Time*, Heidegger points out that in the past being has been thought "in terms of the present-at-hand" and suggests that it must be thought "in terms of the ready-to-hand, which lies closer to us."[36]

Heidegger's highly diverse basic vocabulary is totally original. The reason is that he wishes to think Being as a completely autonomous structure. We may, in anticipation, distinguish now between the later Heidegger's thinking of Being and Burke's by saying that for Heidegger the "ready-to-hand" and the "present-at-hand" can and must be separated; the thinking of Being is a discipline for abolishing the "present-at-hand," or reducing it to secondary ontological status. For Burke that is impossible. Burke cannot abandon theoretical knowledge. That knowledge, where possible, must be revised, humanized. It has been detoxified, made safe by being subordinated within the structure of the act, and unquestionably Burke has, in this way, achieved one of the original objectives of Husserl's reduction. But modern knowledge has not been abolished or divested of a claim to ontological authenticity. Hence, inescapably, the paradox of substance. And it is "an inevitable paradox of definition, an antinomy that must endow the concept of substance with an unresolvable ambiguity, that will be discovered lurking beneath any vocabulary designed to treat motivation by the deliberate outlawing of the word substance." The paradox is unresolvable because it "reflects real paradoxes in the nature of the world itself."[37] Attribution of the paradox to the "nature of the world itself" attests to the unshakable firmness with which Burke conceives the life-world, "man's second nature," as a part of the realm of reality. Burke's paradox, then, corresponds to the "ambiguity" that Sartre finds at the center of the essential nature of the world.[38]

It is possible now to attempt to formulate the relationship between the "paradox of substance" and the "pentad," a relationship which Burke does not thematize but which he says "will become apparent as we proceed." Burke says, "Insofar as you treat of something in terms of its *being* (in contrast for instance in terms of its genesis), by sheer technicality of the treatment you are working in terms of the eternal—outside the category of time." The act, as exemplified in the paradigm of "Creation," occurs at "an intersection of time and the timeless." Burke points out that "in the tradition from which Western philosophy stems, 'form' is the act word par excellence." The pentad is the form generated from the idea of "act." It is, we may infer, "the kind of alienation that accompanies any act of generating or creating, which is an embodiment from within the self." Because the act is the source of form we may see in the pentad the "paradox of substance," a structure of becoming. The individual terms are "attributes of a common ground or substance."[39] I do not see, then, how we can escape the conclusion that the pentad is the paradoxical substance of man, providing we insist that man is a conception that cannot be separated from the conception of the world.

Burke says that the motivation of the work was that his "project needed a grounding in formal considerations logically prior to both the rhetorical and the psychological," that is, the subject which had been his concern for some time and which would be his major preoccupation after *A Grammar of Motives.* The "grounding in formal considerations"—this seems half apologetic, perhaps the first expression of a hesitancy that we may come to understand. But from the first Burke said that the work was "concerned with the basic forms of thought." And what eventually emerges is more than a matter of formal grounding and logical priority: "Our five terms are 'transcendental' rather than formal (and are to this extent Kantian) in being categories which human thought necessarily exemplifies."[40] Burke is, of course, right in seeing a similarity with Kant, but in a period of poststructuralist obsession that similarity becomes misleading. Distinctions must be observed. Kant's transcendentals are a priori; from within subjectivity they impose its character upon experience. What exists beyond experience, *noumena,* cannot be known at all. What most nearly approaches Kant's transcendentals is language itself as Burke and Heidegger conceive it. But language, even if Chomsky is right, is not an a priori; it is not a fixed structure and it does not exist only within subjectivity. The phenomena it produces are "noumena" partly concealed but also partly revealed. So far from being timeless, it creates time. Language opens to the world and history. What Burke describes are the structures of that opening. Our habits of mind tend instantly to reject the notion that structure described in this way might be proposed as ontologically fundamental. We may reject Kant's transcendentals, but granted their fixed and frozen character, we can easily imagine Kant's thinking of them as fundamental. The structures of becoming, however, we tend inevitably to think of as secondary to becoming. We do so because we are intrinsically obsessed by the anthropomorphism of the myth of origins, which Jacques Derrida and George Santayana have helpfully exploded. What we are rejecting is the paradox of substance, which is eventually the necessary burden of a modern philosophy of being.

In the beginning of the work, Burke commits himself to metaphysics. "We hope to make clear the ways in which dialectical and metaphysical issues *necessarily* figure in the subject of motivation. Our speculations, as we interpret them, should show that the subject of motivation is a philosophic one, not ultimately to be solved in terms of empirical science." And "there can be no 'science' of substance." No less indicative of Burke's conviction that he is posing metaphysical foundations is his insistence that "there must be . . . some respect in which act is a *causa sui,* a motive of itself." Unquestionably, in the pentad and the paradox of substance, Burke thinks the Being of the subject and of the object.

It is true that we find in the text the kind of vacillation that apparently caused Burke to write and then to omit from his manuscript "an infinite regress of introductions." Suddenly, after making his most fundamental claim for the structures he has elaborated, Burke says: "Instead of calling them necessary 'forms of experience', however, we should call them the necessary 'forms of *talk about* experience'. For our concern is primarily with analysis of *language* rather than with the analysis of '*reality*'." Indeed, the attempt to understand language is itself justified by its value for social and political therapy. It is "needed if men are to temper the absurd ambitions that have their source in faulty terminologies. Only by such means can we hope to bring ourselves to be content with humbler satisfactions, looking upon the cult of empire as a sickness, be that empire either political or financial."[41] There is no doubt that such political and social concerns are truly dear to Burke, but it is also clear that in 1945 he was worried about the possibility of alienating a positivistically biased readership. He has in *A Grammar of Motives* undertaken two distinct tasks. He has performed a fundamental analysis on a prodigious range of thought. This analysis might have been founded in a Marxian decapitation of Hegelian dialectic. But Burke has developed his own unmistakably metaphysical foundation for this analysis. He is apprehensive lest his metaphysics discredit his analysis. It is none the less true that the structures proposed in *A Grammar of Motives* constitute a metaphysics implicit in, and required by, Burke's thought—and his attitudes—from beginning to end.

chapter 4

Being: The Later Heidegger

COMPARISON of Burke's thought with that of the later Heidegger requires that we have in mind the general character and course of Heidegger's later development, the description of which will be the chief purpose of this chapter. In approaching the later Heidegger it is important to realize that Heidegger and Burke have forced an issue that modern thought on language has not yet resolved. That issue is involved in the later Heidegger's famous statement: "Language is the house of Being."[1] The issue is posed when Heidegger maintains that language is essentially ineffable—"our relation to language is vague, obscure, almost speechless"—and must not be taken as an object.[2] This ineffable power is "the master of man," for "strictly it is language that speaks."[3] Eventually, Heidegger can say, "Language, then, is not a mere human faculty. Its character belongs to the very character of the movement of the face-to-face encounter of the world's four regions," that is, the regions of the "fourfold," the relation of which to the thinking of the Being of the thing will be examined in the next chapter.[4] The decisive fact about language is as follows: "In order to be who we are, we human beings remain committed to and within the being of language, and can never step out of it and look at it from somewhere else. Thus we always see the nature of language only to the extent to which language itself has us in view, has appropriated us to itself."[5]

The question that must arise for us is whether or not there is any significant area of our experience that is not definitively shaped by language. For Burke's part, he is always ready to refer to a distinction between the realm of experience created by language and "reality" (though "reality" is always in quotation marks). For Burke there *is* a material world and we are partly biological and partly cultural (linguistic) beings.[6] Burke can, and often does, entertain all points of view. It remains true, nevertheless, that for Burke, because language saturates experience, there is no objective point of view. No more for Burke than for Heidegger is there such a thing as a bare fact. This takes its greatest significance in that, for Burke as for Heidegger, there is no position or perspective outside of language from which to analyze language. This led Burke in *Attitudes Toward History* to formalize the adoption of the simplest and best known idioms within language for his analytic vocabulary, the idioms of business, sport, crime, folklore—vocabularies of the life-world.[7] This recourse often gives his work a misleadingly folksy flavor. Burke says that any formulation concerning language tends to reveal "the ineffability of linguistic relations" because "any level of conscious explications becomes in a sense but a new level of implications." Burke, like Heidegger, denies in effect that language can be taken as an object. He says, "The ultimate *origins* of language seem to me as mysterious [his simile is pointed] as the origins of the universe itself. One must view it, I feel, simply as a 'given'."[8] Burke too, as we will see later, will deny that language "is a mere human faculty."

We come to perceive in both Heidegger and Burke a kind of solipsism of which there are two aspects. First, language reveals, but as it does so, it also conceals, and what it reveals—"beings" Heidegger would say; "nature" Burke would say—can be known only within limitations and in accord with perspectives imposed by language. The *Ding an sich,* the thing in itself, we never know fully or as an object of stable knowledge. The possibility of our knowing it would depend upon our escaping from language so that we might come to know language and, conceivably then, be able to disentangle what is revealed from it. While Heidegger and Burke deny that we can do this, it must be stressed that what language reveals it reveals in time and history. Hence language for Heidegger and Burke does not become what Fredric Jameson calls "the prison-house of language," which gives rise to the "frozen forms" of a structuralism free of temporality.[9]

Second, and this is especially clear in Burke's work, the life-world is made up of structures which are products of language and which cannot be conceived as determined by what lies outside of language. If we look outside of language for a footing on which to judge these forms, which constitute human culture, we will find that what lies outside always shifts under the moving kaleidoscope of language and can have no authority which is not bestowed upon it by language. The ontological status of both that in which we might find footing and of the cultural forms which we might judge will depend eventually upon the ontological status of language. In the denial of Heidegger and Burke that we can analyze language, apart from its effects, there is implicit protection of the ultimacy of language. The position shared by the two men has for Heidegger the power "to guard the purity of the mystery's wellspring." [10] This does not imply that language is incapable of a critique of language or that within language we may not discriminate. Most of Burke's career has been devoted to such enterprise. However, in Burke the origin of the authority for such a critique must in its turn be derived from choices made available by language. It is partly for this reason that Burke's deconstructions are never quite fatal. In Heidegger, that authority derives from Being itself, but we must in the end question whether Being emerges in his thought with the kind of certainty or specificity that would lend itself reliably to the purpose of discrimination. In fact, in Heidegger's view language has taken the question of discrimination out of our hands. However, and this point will become important later, the solipsism of language found in Burke and Heidegger is in an important sense not a complete solipsism: the object which is the referent of language may be radically determined in its character by language but it remains unmistakably distinguishable from the language which refers to it.

What the solipsism of language and its ontological ultimacy imply is the authenticity of the concept of Being, which is inseparable from language, and of the life-world which is created by language and in which Being is discovered. In this implication, we come to the fact which is central to the thought of Heidegger and Burke. I believe that in some of the directions taken by the later Heidegger we are reminded that it was only here that he came to the fullest development of his conception of language, in whose richness of possibilities there were also dangers.

The relationship of *Being and Time* to the later Heidegger is a subject of some dispute. Heidegger insisted that *Being and Time* is the indispensable foundation of all that follows, and that seems unquestionable. [11] It is also true, however, that Heidegger came increasingly to question and eventually to reject basic aspects of *Being and Time,* and to do so in a way that is crucial for the later work: "The fundamental flaw of the book *Being and Time* is perhaps that I ventured forth too far too early." Heidegger came eventually to the conclusion that Being cannot be thought in "concept and system." *Being and Time* is a systematic work of conceptual thought; it is a work of the kind of discursive thought that characterizes Western philosophy from Plato onward, the essential nature of which Heidegger rejects as representative thinking, which he calls "metaphysics." Heidegger comes to say that "all of the great thinking of the Greek thinkers, including Aristotle, thinks nonconceptually." With the Greeks, especially the pre-Socratics, always as his model, he says, "The thinking that is to come is no longer philosophy, because it thinks more originally than metaphysics—a name identical to philosophy." *Being and Time* had been "fundamental ontology." Later the very term "ontology" is rejected because ontology "does not think the truth of Being and so fails to recognize that there is a thinking more rigorous than the conceptual." The departure from conceptual thought requires a Kierkegaardian "leap," though we are to understand that it is not a leap of faith but of thought: "The leap alone takes us into the neighborhood where thinking resides."[12]

The later conception of "thinking" is closely related to Heidegger's treatment of art. The aesthetics of the past, essentially the Kantian aesthetics, must be abandoned: "On the strength of a recaptured, pristine relation to being we must provide the word 'art' with a new content."[13] This new content is developed primarily in "The Origin of the Work of Art" (1935).[14] In this work, in accord with the abolition of subjectivity and with the conception of Dasein as being-in-the-world, the Kantian idea of the imagination, or of the artist as genius, is not the origin of the work of art. The artist, except as mediating craftsman, disappears: "Art is the origin of the art work and of the artist." The meaning of "art" is a matter of central interest. We are told that "the work as work sets up a world." We will want to consider carefully the following statements: "The art work opens up in its own way the Being of beings." And: "*Art then is the becoming and happening of truth.*" If we now remember that for Heidegger Being is the process of truth as unconcealment (*alētheia*), it becomes clear that it is not possible to distinguish between what Heidegger means by "art" and what he means by "Being." What Being is remains at this point in Heidegger's thought undetermined, and in an addendum to the essay

Heidegger reminds us that he has not attempted to say what art is, explaining: "Reflection on what art may be is completely and decidedly determined only in regard to the question of Being." [15]

The suggestion that the activity of art is the foundational activity of human experience is reinforced in connection with two particulars. It is in the work of art that we come to know for the first time two things—the equipmentality of "equipment" and the earth as "earth." [16] We will see that it is only in the object as equipment (ready-to-hand) that it is possible to think the Being of the "thing" and that in the Being of the "thing" earth is a necessary element (the nature of which will be indicated later). The relevance of the essay to the development of the later Heidegger is also reflected in the fact that the truth of art, like "the thinking that is to come," is dependent upon a "founding leap." A fundamental point, the tremendous importance of which will become clearer as we proceed, is: "*All art . . . is essentially poetry.*" The reason is, first, that "language itself is poetry in the essential sense" and, second, "language alone brings what is, as something that is, into the Open for the first time." [17] Concerning the meaning of "the Open," a Heideggerian term avoided by many commentators, I think there can be no doubt. The correlative statement, based on the causal hypothesis introduced early in this study, would be, "Language causes consciousness and is accountable for all its contents; Heidegger's Open is consciousness." A phenomenological translation of this, close to Heidegger's meaning, would be, "The Open is the scene or stage in-the-world where beings appear." Heidegger's term "clearing," or "lighting" (*Lichtung*), would seem to designate the Open in modes of special ontological authenticity. What the term "consciousness" would have occurring inside the skull, occurs for Heidegger "in-the-world." In another sense the Open and the clearing are the "world." So if it is the poetry of language that first brings beings into the Open, then everything that makes up the content of the work of art is "unconcealed" and shaped by poetry. Furthermore, if it is language as poetry that brings things into the Open, then the implication is that consciousness itself, *authentic* consciousness, we might say, is fundamentally an artistic activity, though Heidegger, who cannot speak of consciousness in a way which would arrogate its contents from "in-the-world," does not say so. This extension of the meaning of art implies the rejection of the Kantian aesthetic, a rejection common to Heidegger and Burke, art for Burke being continuous with life in the continuity of rhetoric. [18]

Clearly the fundamental human activity as artistic activity is close to Heidegger's hope to achieve a kind of thinking that will not be "conceptual" and "representative." "Perhaps," he says, "there is a thinking outside the distinction of rational and irrational still more sober than scientific technology, more sober and thus removed, without effect and yet having its own necessity."[19] Heidegger's most sustained effort to characterize such a thinking is to be found in *What Is Called Thinking?* (1951–52).[20] (In the later Heidegger the word "thinking" always means the thinking of Being.) Heidegger asks what has been the spirit of the conceptual, representative, and metaphysical thinking of the past, and affirms Nietzsche's answer that it has been "revenge."[21] The thinking that is revenge Heidegger will replace with thinking that is "a thanking," for which he finds authentication, as he often does, in etymology: "the Old English noun for thought is *thanc* or *thonc*—a thought, a grateful thought." Such thinking, Heidegger says, "is almost closer to the origins than that thinking of the heart which Pascal, centuries later and even then in conscious opposition to mathematical thinking, attempted to retrieve." From the conception of thinking as thanking there develops terminology basic for the later Heidegger. The word "thinking," says Heidegger, "now speaks in the essential context which is evoked by the words *thanc*, recalling thought, thanks, memory." "Memory" does not mean just the power to recall: "The word designates the whole disposition [of the individual] in the sense of a steadfast intimate concentration on the things that essentially speak to us in every thoughtful meditation. Originally, 'memory' means as much as devotion: a constant abiding with something." And, "Out of the memory, and within the memory, the soul then pours forth its wealth of images—of visions envisioning the soul itself." What Heidegger means by "memory" is very close to what he means by the all-important word "gathering." The "original nature of memory" is "the *gathering* of the constant intention of everything that the heart holds in present being" (my italics). "The thanc, the heart's core, is the *gathering* of all that concerns us, all that we care for, all that touches us insofar as we are, as human being" (my italics). The meaning of "gathering" is also the meaning of "keeping": "Keeping is the fundamental nature and essence of memory."[22] The traditional, discursive thought of the West is logical; it analyzes and orders, and is thus fundamentally dissociational; fundamentally it is nihilism. As philosophy it is "supra-historical knowledge"; it seeks to master history, whether in the mode of Nietzsche or of Marx. What Heidegger calls thinking is a meditation that synthesizes. It effects that synthesis that is the act of *resolve*. In *memory* and *gathering*, "what is past, present, and to come appears in the oneness of its own present being." Because this thought is synthesizing, it "remains open to more than one interpretation" and "multiplicity of meanings is the element in which all thought must move in order to be strict thought." In the synthesizing and polysemous character of thinking lies its affinity with poetry. "When we reflect on poetry, we find ourselves at once in that same element in which thinking moves," and thinking "goes its way in the neighborhood of poetry."[23]

To speak of bringing thinking into the neighborhood of poetry may suggest the "subjectivity" that is a constant danger to Heidegger's thought and to our understanding of his intention. If, for instance, we were to move directly from *Being and Time* to the thinking of the "thing," which will be examined later, and if we took the structures found there as the product of phenomenological observation, we might conclude that the relationship between the early and later Heidegger is not theoretical but practical. It would seem reasonable to imagine that the structures emerging there would be the product of a mind conditioned by a Heideggerian hygiene—the "resolve" by which Dasein achieves authenticity. But such a conception would be disastrous for Heidegger's thought. It would restore the "subject" and "representative thinking" which Heidegger labored from the first to abolish; it would introduce psychological and, in fact, causal factors. Indeed, the danger of subjectivity lurks in the very idea of the "thinking of Being"—in thinking as "subject" and in Being as "object." The dangers are, first, that thinking may be conceived as the agency producing Being and, second, that thinking may be conceived as separate from and independent of Being. Thirteen years after the publication of *Being and Time* Heidegger remarked on the ardors of the project of the thinking of Being subsequent to that work: "the attempt and the path it chose confront the danger of unwillingly becoming another entrenchment of subjectivity."[24]

It has not been sufficiently understood that the necessity of avoiding that danger accounts for the most disturbing conception of the later work. In *Being and Time* the relationship between thinking and Being seems reassuring: "Of course only so long as Dasein *is* . . . 'is there' Being." And: "That there are 'eternal truths' will not be adequately proved until someone has succeeded in demonstrating that Dasein has been and will be for all eternity." And: "Before there was

Dasein there was no truth; nor will there be any after Dasein is no more."[25] Dasein, then, has primacy; Being is dependent on Dasein. But in the later Heidegger, as Father William J. Richardson has pointed out, Being takes on primacy and, more, it takes on initiative:[26] "What calls us [or Being] wants to be thought about according to its nature."—"Being lets beings loose into the daring venture."—The "Being of beings" is "something of which man never is the master, of which man can only be the servant."—"For Being has no equal whatever. It is not brought about by anything else nor does itself bring anything about." The import of the last sentence is indicated by the sentence which immediately follows: "Being never at any time runs its course within a cause-effect coherence."—The independency and initiative of Being has its parallel in statements about beings other than Dasein: "The tree faces us. The tree and we meet one another, as the tree stands there and we stand face to face with it."[27]

Almost inevitably the modern reader assumes that he is dealing here with metaphor. The truth is that to read these statements as metaphorical is to deny Heidegger all that he has attempted to achieve in the later work. It is to assume that his thinking of Being has some literal and logical meaning that is its *real* meaning. In other words, it is to assume that his thinking of Being can be translated back into the normal discourse of Western thought and that Heidegger has not really attempted to escape from "metaphysics." Of our standing "face to face" with the tree, Heidegger says: "This face-to-face meeting is not then one of these 'ideas' buzzing about in our heads. Let us stop here for a moment, as we would to catch our breath before and after a leap. For that is what we *are*, men who have leapt, out of the familiar realm of science and even, as we shall see, out of the realm of philosophy."[28] The independence and initiative of beings and of Being is Heidegger's Kierkegaardian leap of thought. And the leap is for Heidegger not capricious, but a necessity of thought. It must be kept in mind that Heidegger, like Burke, has rejected the autonomy of thought. Thought as autonomous can deal with the idea of Being only in one of two ways. Autonomous thought can become Being, as it does in Hegel, or it can abolish Being, as it does in Nietzsche—the two thinkers in whom Heidegger sees the consummation, the logical completion of "metaphysics." (There is, then, a parallel between the problem of God and the problem of Being.) According to Heidegger, a separation of thought and being and a domination of being by thought occurs first in Plato, in the separation of "idea" and "reality."[29] The logically necessary alternative is that thinking be included within Being: "To surpass the traditional logic does not mean elimination of thought and the domination of sheer feeling; it means a more radical, stricter thinking, a thinking that is part and parcel of being." The effort to sustain the relationship, which is fundamentally the abolition of subjectivity, accounts for much of the complexity of Heidegger's later writing, as in the following, which is perhaps his most succinct statement of the relation between being and thinking: "Thinking belongs to Being itself, insofar as thinking, true to its essence, maintains access to something that never comes to Being as such from just anywhere, but approaches *from* Being itself, indeed as It itself, and 'is' Being, itself *withal*." For Heidegger, as for Burke, hierarchy is implicit in Being: "If being is to disclose itself it must itself have and maintain a rank. . . . What has the higher rank is the stronger."[30]

The suggestion of the power of Being over man is virtually intolerable to Western thinking, for it comes necessarily to the verge, at least, of mysticism: "Before he speaks man must first let himself be claimed again by Being." Furthermore, Being "*requires* a place, a scene of disclosure" and that scene of disclosure is "man." With this Heidegger's relationship between Being and man parallels directly that of Plotinus, just as Burke's conception of form as an alienation of act suggests the conception of *emanation* in Plotinus. The Plotinian configuration is also suggested in the close relationship between "art" and "Being" which has been noted above. However, Heidegger rejects explicitly the mystical and theological implications of a generally Plotinian scheme of things. He does this in his rejection of personalism. The "doctrine of man as a person," Heidegger says, "can thereafter be expressed theologically. *Persona* means the actor's mask through which his dramatic tale is sounded. Since man is the percipient who perceives what is, we can think of him as the *persona*, the mask of, Being." Heidegger rejects this as "metaphysical doctrine." Such a mystical doctrine arises because we persist in asking, with our inveterately metaphysical bias, "*why* being is" and "by what is being caused?"[31]

Within "metaphysics" we ask for logic and cause, and the "overcoming" of "metaphysics" in the idea of the independence and initiative of beings and of Being requires the development of new kinds of relationships that are not logical and causal. We may encounter such a relationship in connection with the concepts of "destinying" and "Enframing" as they are developed in the essays "The Turning" and "The Question Concerning Technology." The destinying that accounts for the fact that Being reveals itself in different ways in different epochs is something which man does not cause and over which he has no control at all. And yet if there is to be an epoch of the Destinying of Being itself, an epoch in which Being unconceals itself as Being, as Heidegger foresees in "The Turning," something is "required of us." What is required is, in fact, the principle of *resolve*, though its effects will not be causal or controlling. The principle of resolve will be observed in that the role of Death in the thinking of the Being of Dasein in *Being and Time* has its corollary in the role of Enframing in the thinking of the Being of the "thing" and the "world."

Enframing (*Gestell*) is Heidegger's name for that "destinying" that has prevailed in the West in all thought following the pre-Socratics and is a principle that unites science and technology. The nature of Enframing, says Heidegger, is to convert everything into a "standing reserve," and, as standing reserve, the object as "thing" disappears. Enframing, says Heidegger, is "one among Being's modes of coming to presence," but it is a mode which poses the danger of Being's being unable to unconceal itself. Enframing is the danger to being, the danger of oblivion. Enframing is a mode of Being, as is for Heidegger the "nothing" of death, but the danger is "Being endangering itself in the truth of its coming to presence." Heidegger says, "Being dismisses and puts away its truth into oblivion in such a way that Being denies its own coming to presence." Facing Technology and Enframing, as in facing death, man is powerless: "Technology, whose essence is Being itself, will never allow itself to be overcome by men. That would mean rather after all, that man was the master of Being." Rather, "man is indeed needed and used for the restorative surmounting of the essence of technology. But man is used here in his essence that *corresponds* to that surmounting." "Corresponds," "corresponding"—this is the new noncausal relationship. For corresponding to occur "man's essence must first open itself to the essence of technology." With this there occurs the "coming to presence of the danger," with which also "there comes to and dwells a favor, namely, the favor of the turning about of the oblivion of Being into the truth of Being." The "bringing to pass of the turning about of oblivion" has the character of an "in-turning" and an "in-flashing," and "in insight, men are the ones which are caught sight of."[32] When man comes into view as freed from the oblivion imposed by technology—much as Dasein comes to authenticity in *Being and Time*—there comes about the possibility of a renunciation parallel with the earlier conception of resolve, by which man affirms death and his finitude in joy. By this renunciation man can come to correspond to the advent of Being.[33] The relationship, then, between man's capacities and Being would seem to be comparable to the universal harmony uniting the monads of Leibniz, on whom Heidegger lectured extensively. The ideas of the initiative of Being and the corresponding of man, invoking respectively Plotinus and Leibniz, are necessary as the means by which the later Heidegger avoids subjectivity. And to the extent that they result from logical necessity, phenomenology gives way in the later Heidegger to speculative philosophy.

Understandably, the reader wants to know more about *corresponding*, to go behind it, to have it explained, and, failing that, he feels that he does not understand Heidegger. What must be understood is that there is no way of translating "corresponding" into a more comprehensible language; there are no concepts from any familiar realm of knowledge that will *explain* corresponding. Heidegger makes that point explicitly.[34] Often the terminology of the later Heidegger must be accepted at face value. His distinctive terms are original; they are the ultimate ligatures of a unique and autonomous intellectual formation. The distinctive terms may be understood only on the basis of their interrelationships, and some of them must be examined as we approach Heidegger's ultimate effort at the thinking of Being.

Heidegger points out that originally the meaning of *logos* "stands in no direct relation to language." From the first, however, its meaning was, for Heidegger, the fundamental function of giving unity, *gathering:* "*Logos* is the steady gathering, the intrinsic togetherness of the essent, i.e., being." Gathering "is never a mere driving-together and heaping up. It maintains in a common bond the conflicting and that which stands apart." Gathering accounts for "unity" which is the "belonging-together of antagonisms. This is the original oneness." "Belonging-together" is another basic term. More specifically, "being and thinking in a contending sense are one, i.e., the same in the sense of belonging-together," and, as we know, they belong-together in *corresponding.* The two words mean essentially the same. Now, it is Being, as "overpowering appearing," that is, the awesome totality of appearances, or beings, which "necessitates the gathering which pervades and grounds being-human," pervades and grounds in the sense that openness to appearances, beings, is what constitutes being human.

Openness, in the language of "metaphysics," would mean capacity for experience. "Man is the site of openness, the there." The later Heidegger departs from the original meaning of logos. The gathering that is necessitated by Being "is first effected in language."[35] The identification of logos and language occurs in the development of the concept of *Saying.*

Saying is a product of Heidegger's culminating thought on language. He sees that "the question of Being will involve us deeply in the question of language," and there "must be a real revolution in the prevailing relation to language."[36] What must be taken into account is the totality of man's saturation with language:

> Man speaks. We speak when we are awake and we speak in our dreams. We are always speaking, even when we do not utter a single word aloud, but merely listen or read, and even when we are not particularly listening or speaking but are attending to some work or taking a rest. We are continually speaking in one way or another. . . . Only speech enables man to be the living being he is as man. It is as one who speaks that man is—man.[37]

That language accounts for what "metaphysics" would call "consciousness" is made quite explicit. "Language speaks." Language is a constant activity of our condition to which we constantly listen: "No matter in what way we may listen besides, whenever we are listening to something we are *letting something be said to us* [Heidegger's italics], and *all perception and conception is already contained in that act*" [my italics]. Heidegger says, "We shall call the being of language in its totality 'Saying'." And Saying is "showing"; it is bringing into unconcealment, into appearance: "Saying is in no way the linguistic expression added to phenomena after they have appeared—rather, all radiant appearance and all fading away is grounded in the showing of Saying." Heidegger says, "the oldest word for the rule of the word thus thought, for Saying, is logos." Logos and language considered in its totality have become one. The full import of this is that "language is the lighting-concealing advent of Being itself." "Saying is the gathering that joins all appearance of the initself manifold of showing which everywhere lets all that is shown abide within itself."[38]

While Heidegger does not make the argument, there are, after all, objective grounds for thinking of language as larger than the individual and as exerting control over him, and, because of the intimate connection for Heidegger between language and Being, one might wish to take the initiative of language as a rationale for Heidegger's conception of the initiative of Being. Such an argument, however, is not conclusive, if only because for the later Heidegger Being is prior to language.

Deferring for later examination Heidegger's thinking of the Being of the "thing," we may move now to his effort to think Being. Since *Being and Time* Heidegger had written a great deal on the history of philosophy and he had treated a wide range of subjects in a way informed by the generalized conception of Being. Unquestionably, he had established what he had hoped for: "a totally new way of thinking about things." [39] All this was in a sense preparatory to the thinking of Being. The "attempt to think Being without beings" Heidegger undertook in the essay "Time and Being" (1962), which significantly reverses the order of things in the title of *Being and Time*.[40]

Of fundamental importance is the fact that Heidegger has abandoned the attempt, apparently intended in *Being and Time*, to think Being in accord with the conception of time as "the horizon of Being." The relationship has changed. It remains true that "Being as *presencing*" (my italics) remains determined as presence by time. Nevertheless, "Being is not a thing, is not in time." Being and time now simply "belong together."[41] And both are in a sense dependent on something else. It turns out that to think Being it is necessary to think something that is logically prior to Being. The central statement is quoted below. The translator has properly left the word *Ereignis* untranslated, for it translates simply as "event," and "event" for Heidegger, as we will see, has a special meaning. There is something, logically prior, which "sends" Being and "extends" time:

> In the sending of the destiny of Being, in the extending of time, there becomes manifest a dedication, a delivering over into what is their own, namely of Being as presence, and of time as the realm of the open. What determines both, time and Being, in their own, that is, in their belonging together, we shall call *Ereignis*, the event of Appropriation. One should bear in mind, however, that "event" is not simply an occurrence, but that which makes any occurrence possible.[42]

We must now consider the meaning of "Appropriation." Heidegger suggested that he hardly intended the essay as an argument of logical coherence. He says at the beginning: "Let me give a little hint on how to listen. The point is not to listen to a series of propositions, but rather to follow the movement of the showing."[43] The truth, however, is that the essay, written long after Heidegger had declared language inadequate to the thinking of Being, proceeds conceptually. Insofar as we are to understand, we must understand "Appropriation." In the earlier essay, "The Way to Language" (1959), Heidegger explains "Appropriation" in this way: "*The moving force in the Showing of Saying is Owning. . . .* This owning which brings them there, and which moves Saying as Showing, we call Appropriation." Appropriation is "*the moving force*" that moves language and thus accounts for the Being of beings. But because to think Being without beings is the purpose of "Time and Being," there is little concern with the role of language in the bringing about of beings. Furthermore, we are now told that we must not think of Appropriation as "an indeterminate power which is supposed to bring about all giving of Being and of time."[44] Heidegger's treatment of Appropriation consists basically in demonstrating that what it is cannot be revealed in logical discourse. The question "What is Appropriation?" becomes a question about the Being of Appropriation, while the logic in which the question is approached requires that Appropriation be antecedent to Being.[45] Eventually it is possible, not to define Appropriation, but only to identify its peculiar properties. The first of these is that "Appropriation withdraws what is most fully its own from boundless unconcealment."[46] This would seem to rest upon Heidegger's earliest explanation of truth, or *alētheia*, as being always both unconcealment and concealment. Another peculiar quality of Appropriation is that it brings "man into his own as the being who perceives Being by standing within true time."[47] In Heidegger's earliest terminology "standing within true time" is achieved by the resolve which establishes authenticity, and man always has at least an ontic perception of Being. Standing within true time, man is "thus Appropriated" and "belongs to Appropriation." But in belonging to Appropriation man is also "assimilated" by Appropriation. This means that man is "admitted to the Appropriation" and "this is why we can never place Appropriation in front of us, neither as something opposite us nor as something all-encompassing."[48] This parallels Heidegger's argument that because we live within langauge we can never know langauge. If we might now argue that in belonging to Appropriation man, in language and in knowing, Appropriates beings, then again a Plotinian configuration of

Heidegger's thought would emerge. That, however, would mean that "Being" *is* language, of which Heidegger never admits, and the text of "Time and Being" does not legitimate such an argument. We have only the argument that because man is "admitted to appropriation" neither discursive argument nor simple statement can "correspond" to Appropriation.[49] Eventually all we can say is: "Appropriation appropriates." In the sentence which immediately follows, Heidegger returns to the point at which his thinking of Being began: "Saying this, we say the Same in terms of the Same about the Same." The Same, says Heidegger, is "the oldest of the old in Western thought: that ancient something which conceals itself in *alētheia.*"[50] In the end, logical discourse can identify Being only as "that ancient something."

At the end of the essay, Heidegger acknowledges that he has not succeeded in escaping from "metaphysics": "The lecture has spoken merely in propositional statement." In effect, Heidegger abandons finally the hope of thinking Being in a way that is communicable in propositional language: "To think Being without being means: to think Being without regard to metaphysics. Yet a regard for metaphysics still prevails even in the intention to overcome metaphysics. Therefore our task is to cease all overcoming, and leave metaphysics to itself." The status of the question of the thinking of Being is indicated in "The End of Philosophy and the Task of Thinking" (1964). "Philosophy," says Heidegger, "is ending in the present age. It has found its place in the scientific attitude of socially active humanity." He asks *"What task is reserved for thinking at the end of philosophy?"* and answers that the remaining task "is only preparatory, not of a founding character." The hope that remains must be interpreted as a hope for "The Turning," for the coming of an epoch of "the destinying of Being," which will replace the destinying of Enframing. Heidegger says, "We are thinking of the possibility that the world civilization which is just now beginning might one day overcome the technological-scientific-industrial character as the sole criterion of man's sojourn."[51] Meantime we must continue the attempt "to think" in a way that escapes from "metaphysics."[52]

As Derrida says, Heidegger wished to remain within "metaphysics."[53] Within metaphysics, however, he failed in his lifelong effort to think Being, and it is as the representative of this failure that he has been canonized by postmodernism. In "The Question of Being," Heidegger in 1955 had declared language to be irredeemably "metaphysics" and had resorted to writing ~~Being~~ in this way, which Derrida calls *sous rature*.[54] Hence, Derrida celebrates Heidegger as achieving the "first writing."[55] What Derrida calls "writing" is a prelinguistic articulation which, he says, underlies all language. We are apparently to understand, however, that writing, or "arche-writing," can be realized—by the very late Heidegger and by Derrida, in such works as *Glas*—in a way that is not translatable into the logical discourse which characterizes all the thought of the past and which continues to prevail in most intellectual communication at the present. Against the background of Heidegger's failure within "metaphysics" and the advent of "writing," Heidegger's style, which was achieved *within* "metaphysics" and for which he at first apologized, has taken on talismanic value.[56] It is in fact an extremely difficult but impressive style, pervasively marked by a profoundly consistent mind and a powerful personality. Unfortunately the power of the style combined with its persistent ambiguities has fostered a guileless valorization of ambiguity which can give rise in modern devotees to such ecstasies as the following: "Heidegger seeks to harness and rekindle the numinous energy of the source. He wants to disclose and unconceal. He aims to act out and produce truth before our eyes. In such moments, Heidegger takes analysis beyond explanation toward vision: he performs truth. The rapture and astonishment and primal wonder which result sweep Heidegger as well as his readers along. The impression that language speaks, not the author, is strong—very strong."[57] One's response to this is, apparently, a matter of faith. I continue in the confidence that Heidegger's permanent accomplishment occurred within "metaphysics" and that, with some difficulty, it can be clearly explicated. We must next consider Heidegger's thinking of the "thing."

chapter 5

The "Thing" and Questions of Faith

BURKE, at the beginning of his systematic enterprise, seems to have undertaken the thinking of Being and to have abandoned it, at least for the time being, to turn to the thinking of the Being of the subject and of the object in the pentad and the paradox of substance. We have now observed the point at which Heidegger, at the end of his career, abandons the discursive thinking of Being. But before arriving at this point, Heidegger too had undertaken the thinking of the Being of the object, of the "thing," in which we will observe further parallels with the thought of Burke.

First, a few terms must be clarified. In the essays "The Thing" and "Building Dwelling Thinking" Heidegger introduces "*the four-fold*," which is the "simple oneness" of "earth and sky, divinities and mortals." Of the four terms, only "mortals" would seem immediately clear. We may say that earth is matter, material, providing we keep in mind that it is matter only as it can be known phenomenologically, within the life-world. Relevant to the term "divinities," Heidegger, building upon, and away from, Nietzsche, comments upon the death of God: "That place of God can remain empty." Heidegger maintains that "the now-empty authoritative realm of the suprasensory and the ideal world can still be adhered to." It would seem then that, within the "fourfold," we may take "divinities" as referring either to the gods or to the empty place from which they have disappeared. The special quality of the "thing," such as a bridge, for instance, is that it "gathers" and within that gathering the divinities are present "whether we explicitly think of, and visibly *give thanks for,* their presence, as in the figure of the saint on the bridge, or whether that divine presence is obstructed or even pushed wholly aside." Concerning the sky, we may note that in the passage above, building away from Nietzsche, the "suprasensory" and "the ideal world" are closely associated in "the now-empty realm." In "Memorial Address," in *Discourse on Thinking,* Heidegger equates "the free air of the high heavens" with "the open realm of the spirit." [1] It would seem permissible, then, to think of "sky" as "the ideal world" and, in some sense, the home of the gods. I believe this is also supported by a passage in the final chapter of *Being and Time* which seems to associate consciousness and the life-world with sight, brightness, the sun, and time, which is "the horizon of Being." [2] This interpretation of the "fourfold" will be more understandable and more credible when we consider Heidegger's "The Turning" later on.

The focus of the thinking of the "thing" as being in "Building Dwelling Thinking" is a bridge. The central passage is as follows:

The bridge *gathers* to itself in its *own way* earth and sky, divinities and mortals.

Gathering or assembly, by an ancient word of our language is called "thing." The bridge is a thing—and, indeed, it is such as the gathering of the fourfold which we have described. [3]

In the present context it is of interest that everything here turns upon an act—the "gathering"—or what in nonphenomenological parlance would be seen as a projection of an act of consciousness. It is important too that the "ready-to-hand" as equipment, which has become the focus of the thinking of being, presupposes, of course, an activity, and for Heidegger human action is an act in Burke's sense. It is the act which bestows upon the thing its being: "To use something is to let it enter into its essential nature, to keep it safe in its essence." In *Being and Time,* Heidegger discusses the act, drawing upon Max Scheler, to explain why Dasein is not a thing: "Essentially the person exists only in the performance of intentional acts." In the thinking of the Being of the jug, in "The Thing," the Event is introduced in a way that turns upon a human act: "The jug's jug-character consists in the poured gift of the pouring out."[4] Heidegger treats the outpouring as of water and as of wine, both as for drink and as libation. The fourfold is developed poetically:

> The spring stays on in the water of the gift. In the spring the rock dwells, and in the rock dwells the dark slumber of the earth, which receives the rain and the dew of the sky. In the water of the spring dwells the marriage of sky and earth. It stays in wine given by the fruit of the vine.[5]

The thinking of the being of the thing culminates as follows:

> In the gift of the outpouring that is drink, mortals stay in their own way. In the gift of the outpouring that is a libation, the divinities stay in their own way, they who receive back the gift of giving as the gift of the donation. In the gift of the outpouring, mortals and divinities each dwell in their different ways. Earth and sky dwell in the gift of the outpouring. In the gift of the outpouring earth and sky, divinities and mortals dwell *together all at once.* These four, at one because of what they themselves are, belong together. Preceding everything that is present, they are enfolded into a single fourfold.
>
> The gift of the outpouring dwells in the simple singlefoldness of the four.[6]

The thinking of the being of the thing is the thinking of the being of the world: "The world grants to things their presence. Things bear world. World grants things." Heidegger maintains that he must not be conceived as attempting to restore an older order of consciousness or older concepts but as thinking of Being totally anew: "Not only are things no longer admitted as things, but they have never yet at all been able to appear to thinking as things." They perhaps have not appeared to "thinking," but we may look for an origin of the fourfold—within Heidegger's own intellectual experience and within history as he interprets it. We find it, fifteen years before Heidegger's thinking of the "thing," at the center of Heidegger's conception of the character of pre-Socratic culture in which *physis*, according to Heidegger, was identified with Being. The "essence and character" of *physis* "are defined as that which emerges and endures."[7]

Hence *physis* originally encompassed heaven as well as earth, the stone as well as the plant, the animal as well as man, and it encompassed human history as the work of men and the gods; and ultimately and first of all, it meant the gods themselves as subordinated to destiny.[8]

If modern conceptions of language and consciousness can conflate plant, animal, and stone with "earth," what remains is the fourfold. And by implication the pre-Socratic fourfold is what has disappeared from the modern world: "We have said that the world is darkening. The essential episodes of this darkening are: the flight of the gods, the destruction of earth, the standardization of man, the pre-eminence of the mediocre." The Greek origins of the conception of the fourfold will at one point provide at least indirect support for the description of homologies between Heidegger's thinking of the thing and Burke's conception of the pentad.

As has been pointed out, act is an essential concept in the thinking of the thing, the act being the endowment of mortals. And "When we say mortals," says Heidegger, "we are then thinking of the other three along with them by way of the simple oneness of the four."[9] *Earth* corresponds to Burke's "scene," the area of materialism. *Sky* corresponds to "agent" as the area of idealism. Divinities corresponds to "purpose," the area of mysticism. Of Burke's pentad, there is lacking only "agency," which may be subsumed under "scene" (materialism). Heidegger's construct comes into startling conjunction with the pentad in the light of Joseph P. Fell's discussion of the fourfold. According to Fell, the elements of the fourfold, like the elements of the pentad, correspond to Aristotle's causes. Furthermore, thinking that seeks to ground itself in any one of the members of the fourfold destroys the event and the place which bring about and constitute the scene of the thinking of the fourfold, the thinking of the Being of the thing and of the world.[10] The import of the fourfold is that of the pentad.

These correspondences between the central structures of the later Heidegger and of Burke must be considered along with others. Fell says, "If language incorporates in itself the mental-spiritual-imperceptible, and if 'things' themselves are always meaning-beings or linguistic-things, then language always bonds the 'heavenly' to the 'earthly'." In *Being and Time*, Heidegger says that perception "amounts to interpretation in the broadest sense." In the later Heidegger, "The word alone gives being to the thing." In other words, every perception is a coincidence of an "object" and language (culture). "The 'phenomenon' of phenomenology," says Fell, "occurs as precisely this original togetherness." Dramatism, says Burke, "aims always to make us sensitive to the 'ideas' lurking in 'things'." Heidegger's "thing" as a "gathering" of the fourfold is a coincidence of object with language and culture. If we assumed, as does Burke, that a part of the culture that necessarily inheres in this coincidence is theoretical knowledge, then the fourfold would become Burke's paradox of substance. Heidegger's project, indeed, is precisely the exclusion of theoretical knowledge from the "gathering" that is the "thing." By comparison, then, Burke's thinking of being is a compromise, an inescapable compromise, he would maintain. On another point, however, Burke and Heidegger are in agreement: the "thingness" of the thing is more primordial than its dissolution by theoretical knowledge and cannot be obliterated as the underlying structure of experience. The destiny of the West in which the fourfold is not known, Fell explains, is "only the fourfold's greatest possible self-dissimulation." Fell continues, "This means that the fourfold is still present in its absence, that it is present as its absence." Burke, dealing with the test case, says that the paradox of substance is an "antinomy" that "will be discovered lurking beneath any vocabulary designed to treat motivation by the deliberate outlawing of the *word* for substance." [11]

We must not leave Heidegger's fourfold without considering very special characteristics of "earth." Insofar as "earth" is associated with matter, the life-world would seem to have given way to the introduction of theoretical knowledge. Contrarily, Heidegger's intent is that "earth" be conceived phenomenologically, as phenomena, as life-world. Earth "shatters every attempt to penetrate into it." Every scientific or theoretical approach to it, "every merely calculating importunity," turns "into a destruction." And yet there is something peculiar about the way in which "earth" *appears*. It appears only in a unique relationship to other phenomena. In "equipment" generally, the material disappears into usefulness. The material appears only as it becomes subordinate to, functional or instrumental within, another kind of appearance, for instance, that of the work of art. In the temple, as a work of art, the material appears: "The temple-work, in setting up a world, does not cause the material to disappear, but rather causes it to come forth for the very first time and to come into the Open of the work's world." This peculiarity of "earth" would seem to be consistent with Gadamer's statement that "earth" is "that out of which everything comes forth and into which everything disappears."[12] This in turn is coherent with Fell's argument that "earth" is introduced to provide a necessary grounding of the phenomenological world, to give it validity, reality, not as its causal origin, but as sharing what Fell calls "a precedent community *of nature.*" Hence "earth" is not Kant's noumenon, not the thing-in-itself, but takes the place of noumenon as ground.[13] We will soon discover in Burke a comparable effort to ground and authenticate Being.

One may not pretend that the relationship between the Being of man and the advent of Being in the later Heidegger is entirely satisfactory. Man only corresponds; furthermore, "his essence is to be the one who waits." On the other hand, "*How* must we think?" is a relevant question, and "thinking is genuine activity, genuine taking a hand, if to take a hand means to lend a hand to the essence, the coming to presence, of Being." Man is in some sense "the shepherd of Being." But what is the role of thinking? Of *corresponding* Heidegger says, "*This primal corresponding,* expressly carried out, *is thinking.*" If thinking is only a corresponding, how can it "lend a hand"? How can man be needed and used? Eventually the coming to pass of a "destinying of Being," which Heidegger foresees as an unquestionable possibility, is not something which we can expect to understand: "When and how it will come to pass after the manner of a destinying no one knows. Nor is it necessary that we know." "Only when man, as the shepherd of Being, attends upon the truth of Being can he expect an arrival of a destinying of Being and not sink to the level of a mere wanting to know."[14] What disturbs us, what we might unpresumptuously want to know, is how Heidegger can know.

The question concerning the relationship of the early and the later Heidegger is parallel to the question of the relationship between Burke's pentad and his paradox of substance. In both cases we are concerned with the relationship between the Being of the subject and the Being of the object. Obviously the relationship for Burke is close, but it is not clear that the two are identical. The paradoxical character of substance might be seen to disappear in the pentad. If the freedom of the act is to be insisted on, then are not the deterministic implications of the theoretical knowledge based on scene (materialism) simply overriden, declared illusionary, forbidden? Or is it the case that the paradox of substance in the experience of things is a paradox that must totally infest our minds as the acknowledgment of the equally authentic claims of freedom and determinism? Burke comes closest to affirming the latter conception in saying that there are "real paradoxes in the nature of the world itself." [15]

We have yet to follow Heidegger and Burke into those areas of their thought where positivistic habits of mind will be, or may seem to be, most inhibiting. I will not pretend to resolve the question as to whether or not the later Heidegger arrives at a religious or mystic position. Werner Brock assures us that Heidegger's use of such terms as "angels" and "the gods" are to be taken literally. [16] Richardson finds that the later Heidegger uses the word "God" in a way that is "conscientiously and doggedly atheistic." [17] John Macquarrie is "unwilling to call Heidegger either a theist or an atheist." [18] Among later critics more agree with Richardson in denying Heidegger's supernaturalism or mysticism, though some of them reject Richardson's observation that the later Heidegger departs from *Being and Time* in the introduction of the idea of the initiative of Being. [19] I have argued above that the idea of the initiative of Being became necessary in order to preserve coherence with the very foundations of the thought of *Being and Time.* This would not deny that what Richardson calls a "turn" was indeed a turn, but it would find the turn's basis in speculative philosophy rather than in an access of mystic insight. My argument would be in harmony with Richardson's opinion on the question of Heidegger and religion.

Both the question of the "turn" in Richardson's sense and the separate question of a mystic faith would seem to become crucial in the essay "The Turning" (1949), which was not available to Richardson at the time of his magisterial study of Heidegger. [20] Some aspects of this essay have been considered above. In this essay Heidegger sees, as did Burke in 1935, the ending of the modern age. [21] What Heidegger foresees, however, is much more; it is an ending of the "destinying" of Enframing which begins with Plato. As pointed out above, Heidegger foresees the possibility that the destinying of Enframing will be replaced by a destinying of Being: "the surmounting of a destinying of Being . . . each time comes to pass out of the arrival of another destinying." [22] Somewhat alarmingly, the arrival of the destinying of Being will contain the possibility of the return of "the god." [23] What is necessary is authenticity, much as Heidegger has characterized it from the first, though he does not now use the word, and with authenticity man may *correspond:*

In this corresponding man is gathered into his own [*ge-eignet*], that he, within the safeguarded element of the world, may, as the mortal, look out toward the divine. Otherwise not; for the god also is—when he is—a being and stands as a being within Being and its coming to presence, which brings itself disclosingly to pass out of the worlding of the world.[24]

The tone of the essay seems to make it a prayer for the advent, and in such a passage as that just quoted Heidegger may seem to have abandoned himself to supernatural prophesy, but his position may be rationalized on the basis of two considerations. On the one hand, he may be seen as a practical observer and evaluator of historical currents. On the other, as we know, the life-world is real, which means that every cultural manifestation must be considered as a manifestation of Being: the god "is—*when* he is" [my italics]. This rationalization, if we remember that "thinking" for Heidegger is always the thinking of Being, would seem to be supported by Heidegger's insistence as late as 1954 upon the following: "The unconditional character of faith, and the problematic character of thinking, are two spheres separated by an abyss."[25] It is also true, however, that the text of "The Turning" supports Richardson's implication that the later Heidegger makes progress toward a supernaturalistic faith without arriving there. Richardson says that the question of the infinitude of Being in the later Heidegger "must be left open."[26] Whatever Heidegger's conception of the ontological status of "the gods," in a statement published, by agreement, after his death he said, "Only a god can save us."[27] This must be understood as an expression of some hope.

We have seen Burke move toward the establishment of a firm and clear-cut metaphysical position and then waver from that possibility. I think that to understand this we must not abandon Burke to positivism but keep in mind the following statement of 1935: "Men build their cultures by huddling together nervously loquacious, at the edge of an abyss."[28] It would seem that for Burke the possibility of the reality of the life-world is always undermined, not by counterclaims of reality, but by a preoccupation with the abyss—which seems a standing rebuke to the possibility of any reality—and a need for something more. Heidegger, too, talks of the "abyss."[29] But he writes: "In the age of the world's night, the abyss of the world must be experienced and endured. But for this it is necessary that there be those who reach into the abyss."[30] Burke, never comfortable with the ultimacy of the life-world, reached eventually into the abyss, grappling for a foundation. In *A Rhetoric of Motives* (1950) Burke writes, "And if we go through the verbal to the outer limits of the verbal, the superverbal would comprise whatever might be the jumping-off place. It would be not nature minus speech, but nature as the ground of speech, hence nature as itself containing the principle of speech. Such an inclusive nature would be more-than-verbal rather than less-than-verbal." Later in the work he develops this further: "'Man' arises out of an extra-human ground. His source is, as you prefer, 'natural', or 'divine', or (with Spinoza) both. In any case, the scene out of which he emerges is *ultimate*. And in this respect it must be 'super-personal', quite as it must be 'super-verbal'. For it contains the principle of personality, quite as it contains the principle of verbalizing."[31] The possible implications of this are awesome. We may, for instance, ask such questions as the following: If personality, which is eventually the product of language, is a principle contained in nature, then is not the principle of the totality of past and present cultural configurations, which are all products of language, contained in the ultimate ground out of which man emerges? Are not *all* cultural configurations thus authenticated? Will not another small step or two carry us to a conception of God, the world, and man such as that proposed by Pierre Teilhard de Chardin, among others?[32]

In Burke there is hardly a hint of such questions. The argument stops where it begins, with the articulation of the proposition: the "extra-human ground" simply "contains the principle of personality, quite as it contains the principle of verbalizing." Implications are mentioned to be dismissed—"as you prefer." It can hardly be that the opening and abrupt closing of the argument is to be explained by a faltering of Burke's tireless imagination or a failure of his apparently limitless intellectual resources. Then why does he leave us on this knife-edge border of a unifying metaphysics?

The idea that we have our origins in the extra-human ground lends itself easily to mythic elaboration, but it must be insisted that nothing in the idea itself requires such an elaboration. The idea is simply the result of the fact that in the light of what we know generally about how things come about, it is more reasonable to conclude that the human emerges from its extra-human setting than to conclude that the human comes into human being spontaneously, with no cause or origin whatever. The idea of itself cannot produce a myth; rather it requires a rejection of a persistent myth of the nineteenth and twentieth centuries, the existentialist myth of the spontaneity and autonomy of man. There can be no doubt, however, that the idea of a link with the extra-human has inevitable attitudinal effects. Existentialism dispels mystery: man creates himself; rationality, to that extent, is autonomous and secure. The truth is that we know nothing of ultimate origins, but we know that there are beginnings. The link with the extra-human means that however much we, like Pascal, may be frightened by "those empty spaces," there is a sense in which we are coherent with what we are not. Looking beyond the human, we despair in the absence of the human and recognize that there is a mystery we must bear and that we must bear it either with anguish or with gratitude. The link with the extra-human is the ground of Burke's "piety."

Furthermore the questions and objections posed above are an effort to go to the end of the line and assume, in fact, that we have already been there. As far as it goes, the argument concerning the "principle of language" and the "principle of personality" (and these are inseparable for Burke) is logically valid, even necessary. It is, indeed, valid and necessary—providing that the appearance of man on earth is not an accident. Here we discover a possible explanation of the somewhat surprising fact that Darwin appears among the chiefly philosophical writers who are deconstructed in *A Grammar of Motives*, and we may suspect that Burke's approach to Darwin is not totally without polemical intent.[33] The result of Burke's analysis is to put in question Darwin's basic principle of natural selection, whereby the origin of species becomes accidental. Burke's argument, essentially, is that he finds Darwin fluctuating within the agency-purpose ratio and, especially, the agent-scene ratio.[34] Darwin's virtually "perfect" materialism is found "slipping into references to *purpose.*" He moves also, argues Burke, from scene (materialism) to agent and thus "we find in his doctrines an idealistic stress." One may protest that while Burke's treatment of particular wording is valid, it cannot possibly do justice to Darwin's argument on the whole, and Burke acknowledges that Darwin's "conscious intention seems purely materialistic."[35] Burke's treatment of Darwin is perhaps the least persuasive of all his deconstructions, and if we are justified in relating it to his conception of language and the "extra-human ground," it is at best a negative argument.

The point is that for Burke, as for Heidegger, language is not "a mere human faculty," though this does not mean that either man conceives language as in any sense a supernatural agency. Language, and therefore personality, must be grounded in an ultimate extra-human ground if the world created by language is not to be a dream and, because a dream, a bad dream; if the life-world is not to be pure illusion. With the argument of the extra-human ground we come also to a parallel with Heidegger's grounding "world" in "earth" without permitting causal relationship to connect them.

Burke's limited metaphysics in his restrained and reticent affirmation of the extra-human ground may be seen to underlie his equally restrained and quite secular treatment of mysticism "in its pure state" in *A Rhetoric of Motives*. Mystic ecstasy, says Burke, has a neurological basis, but the mystic interprets it as knowledge, "telling him of a 'truth' beyond the realm of logical contradictions, and accordingly best expressed in terms of the oxymoron." Then Burke says, "And, indeed, why would it not be 'knowledge'? For if the taste of a new fruit is knowledge, then certainly the experience of a rare and felicitous physical condition would be knowledge too, a report of something from outside the mind, communication with an ultimate, unitary ground." It cannot escape us that if Heidegger's nonconceptual thinking of Being is a nontheistic mysticism, Burke has partially authorized it here. Burke again hurries to allay the positivistic qualms of his readers, but this time his reassurance is itself qualified: "When considering mysticism and its 'fragments', we should attempt to account for *as much as possible* in purely naturalistic terms" [my italics]. Burke points out that there are many "*Ersatzmystiken,*" for instance, the mysticisms of speed, sex, money, crime, drugs, war."[36] There is both an authentic and an inauthentic mysticism. Such "substitute mysticisms," however, are distinguished from true mysticism: "the test . . . is the transforming of means into ends." Though "mysticism is no rare thing," mysticism "in its pure state is rare. And its secular analogues, in grand and gracious symbolism, are rare. But the need for it, the itch is everywhere. And by hierarchy it is intensified."[37] From this Burke moves to the final paragraph of *A Rhetoric of Motives*, which begins as follows: "But since, for better or worse, the mystery of the hierarchic is forever with us, let us, as students of rhetoric, scrutinize its range of entrancement, both with dismay and in delight."[38] And "finally" says Burke—which means perhaps "most importantly"—we should observe one special motive. The description of this motive rises to benediction, almost an invocation. This is the motive that attains its ultimate identification in the thought not of universal holocaust, but of the universal order—as with the rhetorical and dialectic symmetry of the Aristotelian metaphysics, whereby all classes of beings are hierarchally arranged in a chain or ladder or pyramid of mounting worth, each kind striving towards the perfection of its kind, and so towards the kind next above it, while the strivings of the entire series head in God as the beloved cynosure and sinecure, the end of all desire.[39]

The tone here is strikingly similar to that of the final paragraph of Heidegger's "The Turning": "May the world in its worlding, be the nearest of all nearing that nears, as it brings the truth of Being to man's essence, and so gives man to belong to the disclosing bringing-to-pass that is a bringing into its own."[40] It cannot be too much emphasized that if contemporary disdain of Burke's prayerful peroration is necessary, it is disdain for hierarchy, for a capacity for delight as well as dismay, and not for supernaturalism. If there is any reason why Burke's piety here should be put in some special perspective, that can be accomplished by pointing out that five years later Burke would publish his massive "deconstruction" of Hebraic and Christian myth in *The Rhetoric of Religion*. We may also consider Burke's only extended references to a work of Heidegger, the essay "What Is Metaphysics?"

For both Burke and Heidegger the concept of the negative is of great importance, though for Heidegger another word is required. In "What Is Metaphysics?" Heidegger develops the theme of "the nothing."[41] Heidegger says the nothing is not "non-being": "we posit it as being." It "is more original than the 'not' of negation." The nihilation of the nothing is something other than the negation of thought, and its effects we know—in "unyielding antagonism and stinging rebuke," in "galling failure" and "bitter privation."[42] We are brought before the nothing itself in "anxiety," which may be explained in this way: though we cannot think the totality of "the ensemble of beings," we do nevertheless "find ourselves stationed in the midst of beings that are revealed somehow as a whole"; in anxiety "the nothing makes itself known with beings and in being expressly as a slipping away of the whole." Anxiety and the slipping away of the whole are a constant of Dasein and constitute its "being held out into the nothing." This is a "surpassing of beings as a whole. It is transcendence." It is thus that the nothing "brings Dasein for the first time before beings as such." In other words, it is only through the transcendence of beings that beings can be known. The nothing "is manifest in the ground of Dasein" and "reveals itself as belonging to the Being of beings."[43] The nothing saturates existence.

"What Is Metaphysics?" is the only work of Heidegger's that we know Burke to have read. Burke first discusses this work in "A Dramatistic View of the Origins of Language."[44] Burke's treatment of "origins" is limited to a brief development of the proposal that language began as a "positive pre-negative" in the form of a "demonstrative" that was transformed into a "hortatory negative."[45] This long essay, divided into eighteen chapters, is a very wide-ranging exploration of the constant role of the negative in language as illustrated in philosophy, theology, religion, literature, and human experience. We know the negative in the concept of death, in the restrictive claims of the ownership of property, in "mortification," in the instinctive recoil from certain images, in "victimage, or purification by sacrifice," in "completion, perfection," resulting from "linguistic resources whereby local problems of order become translated into grandly Universal replicas—supernatural, metaphysical, or naturalistic."[46] At another level the negative pervades all experience because "symbol-using demands a feeling for the negative" and "a specifically symbol-using animal will necessarily introduce a symbolic ingredient into every experience." Burke follows Bergson in the idea that the negative does not exist in nature and considers it "a peculiarly linguistic resource," but he also entertains the possibility that the ability for the negative is prior to language: "There might even be a sense in which we could derive the linguistic faculty itself from the ability to use the Negative *qua* Negative."[47] Thus far, Burke's conception of the negative is a closely corresponding positivistic version of Heidegger's nothing. It brings Burke close to Sartre's conception of consciousness as nothingness, which is, of course, derived from Heidegger, and like Sartre, Burke here treats the later Heidegger as an expression of mysticism.[48] Toward Heidegger's nothing, however, Burke's attitude is complex.

Burke treats "What Is Metaphysics?" in a chapter entitled "Negative Theology." It is, he says, "a diabolically ingenious essay" in which Heidegger "offers a new variant of that very old dialectical resource whereby the sum total of Being is said to be grounded in Nothing." Burke begins with, as he admits, a heavy metaphysical joke at Heidegger's expense, turning on the fact that Heidegger has converted "nothing" into a verb: "The Ultimate Nothing (*Nichts*) can *enact* its identity; for it can non-do (*nichten*). Or, heavily cavorting, we might translate the verb *nichten* into English thus: *Things* can *be;* and their Being is grounded in *Nothing*'s ability to *noth.*" In addition, Burke looks for a possible psychological reduction of Heidegger's position. This is based on Burke's theory that the "negative *Command* is prior to the purely *Propositional* negative." If you can accept that, he says, "you see a possibility that the metaphysician could be rediscovering, through the labyrinthine virtuosity of his dialectic, the respect and awe of the original No, communicated to him as a child by parents who represented the principle of personal authority." Concerning Heidegger's *Angst,* Burke looks for a sociological explanation: "a terminology essentially metaphysical would also incline to interpret as purely metaphysical any kind of uneasiness stemming from the *social order.*" And *Angst* may also be the result of intellectual experience "when the thought of ultimate questions makes one feel the underpinning of one's beliefs melting away." However, Heidegger's "nothing" is not thus finally dismissed. "Even if we agree with Heidegger's views . . ." says Burke—and he would seem to be holding open that possibility for himself as much as for his readers.[49] We might conclude that Burke is as ambivalent or as shy about Heidegger's metaphysics as he is about his own, but it also must be acknowledged that his discussion here simply puts into practice the principle of multiple motivation systematized in Burke's pentad: "When confronting the verbal tactics of negative theology, we would always stress the purely linguistic elements operating here. At the same time, there is nothing in our position requiring us to deny the possibility that language, with its basic No, is grounded in a transcendent ground."[50] And Burke goes on to recognize that his own reach into the abyss—"language derives from the realm of a 'more-than-language'"—is harmonious with the "transcendent motive" of "negative theology" generally.[51] Burke returns to Heidegger's "nothing" nine years later in *The Rhetoric of Religion.* While cautioning against the tendency of Heidegger and Sartre to reify the negative, he says that "logology would admonish us to take Heidegger's comedy seriously."[52] He now affirms Heidegger's position, making no reference to its metaphysical validity, but seeing in it the expression of a perhaps universal and inescapable psychological condition:

For if man is the symbol-using animal, and if the ultimate test of symbolicity is an intuitive feeling for the principle of the nega-

tive, then such "transcendental" operations as the Heideggerian idea of "Nothing" may reveal in their purity a kind of
Weltanschauung that is imperfectly but inescapably operating in
all of us.[53]

This is followed by a sentence in which Burke epitomizes a lifelong agon that would make nihilistic rigor compatible with meaning:
"Thus, where positivism would simply dismiss such operations as
sheer nonsense, Logology must watch them as carefully as a Freudian
psychologist watches the nonsense of a patient's dreams."[54] Perhaps
the purpose of this is to reassure us. It might mean that logology is
only a more tolerant, more curious, and more analytic positivism.
However, if that *Weltanschauung* derives from the extra-human ground,
it may mean that with enough caution about the silliness of the dream,
of the mysticism, we may derive from mysticism a quite secular truth
about the human condition, a truth that transcends the reach of
positivism and, we may note, that concomitantly transcends the "metaphysics" which Heidegger had eventually to abandon to attempt to
think Being free of language.

chapter 6

Conclusion: The Necessary Metaphysics

BECAUSE so much attention has now been given to demonstrating the similarities between the basic thought of Heidegger and Burke, it may be important to recall that most of the panoply of devices by which Heidegger labored to isolate and secure his world of Being have no equivalent in Burke and that most of Burke's efforts have been devoted to the exploration of the symbolic world rather than to the attempt to arrive at a foundation in the ways which have been examined here. Despite the similarities, the distance between them is very great. No one has done more than Burke to reveal and caution against the pitfalls of language, the constant possibilities it offers for error, the seductions, the dangers, but he remains firmly entrenched within what Heidegger calls "metaphysics." This means simply that although he insists upon the limitations of reason, he is firmly committed to the value and necessity of logical discourse. This fact marks the gulf between Burke and the later Heidegger. The fact remains that when Burke, for whom language came before philosophy, looked for foundations, he was drawn unerringly toward the structures which Heidegger, beginning in philosophy, discovered in language.

The differences in their thought become more conspicuous when their philosophies of Being are seen in larger perspective. Heidegger's effort is to construct an autonomous world of Being that is vastly comprehensive and internally coherent. This world of Being is to usurp entirely the world of theory—the "metaphysics" of the West and of science—and to deprive it of its claims to ontological primacy. The preservation of the autonomy of the world of Being requires that it in some way be grounded. In the later Heidegger this is achieved in the concept of Earth. The problem is that Earth must be in some way connected with matter, which is a concept of Western "metaphysics," but this connection we can never hope to understand because causal relationship is excluded. Being is primary and the "metaphysics" of the West can have only derivative status.

Burke's strategy is in sharp contrast to that of Heidegger. His intent is not to supplant the civilization of the past but to modify it in a way that will ensure its continual change through historical continuity. His strategy is to establish Being within the world and on the basis of minimal claims. While the internal coherence of his thought is intact, his concept of Being depends for its validity upon its external coherence with the widest possible range of thought. Though the implications that might be derived from science are sharply curtailed, the claim of science to ontological validity is not denied. Science, within its proper sphere, is firmly based in the extra-human ground. Burke's strategy is to give to Being an ontological status equal to that of science, an equality that is implicit in the paradox of substance.

In various respects the two writers have polar relationships. Burke defined Being in order to be able to think—about language and human affairs; Heidegger's entire life of thinking was devoted to the defining of Being. The two thinkers have different intellectual affinities. In Burke we are a step, though a decisive step, away from positivism. In Heidegger we are a step away from German idealism; Theodore W. Adorno calls Heidegger's thought a "disguised idealism."[1] Burke describes "dramatism" as "realism," in the Scholastic sense of the word.[2] In the works of the two men we experience intellectual climates that are alien to each other. This is reflected in language. In Heidegger a single monolithic terminology is repeated with hypnotic effect. Burke's tendency is to generate new terminology for every occasion. Heidegger's vocabulary draws upon archaic sources. Burke more frequently adapts contemporary vocabularies to new purposes, with an effect that tends to minimize the reification inherent in language. The worlds of the two writers take their contrasting characters from contrasting focal concerns. Burke's thought turns on the "act," the central vitality; Heidegger's thought turns on "authenticity" as an embrace of death. Moving from Heidegger to Burke, we move from gloom to gaiety, to a comic spirit of great integrity.

Heidegger said, "We are too late for the gods and too early for Being."[3] Meanwhile—and however that may be—the systematic focus of his thought serves to illuminate the foundational character of Burke's thought. What must remain inevitably attractive in Burke's metaphysics is the extraordinary economy of the means by which he has eluded nihilism, the slenderness of his demands on our credulity. Centrally we must accept the concept of the "act." The argument that the act is the product of an infinite, meaning an incomprehensibly large, number of causes might sustain suspension of even positivistic disbelief. We need to believe also that the paradox of substance "reflects real paradoxes in the nature of the world itself." The fact that we must accept both Newton's and Einstein's physics would seem to support that possibility. Then we must be able to believe that the extra-human ground "contains the principle of personality, quite as it contains the principle of verbalizing." Personality is not the problem here, because for Burke personality is defined by the capacity for choice, the basis for which is language. What we hesitate over is the idea that the principle of language is contained within the extra-human ground. Our hesitation is grounded in the deeply rooted conviction that the principle of natural selection means that man is an accident. The notion is encouraged by our general sense of cosmic alienation. But if man is an accident it is only because the origin of every species is an accident. The fact remains that Darwinism and modern linguistic thought have not yet been reconciled. There is a widespread tendency to consider language as totally determinative of man. While we might like to believe that natural selection would discover advantages for survival in language, it might as easily be argued that language would at some times pose profound dangers for the species, the modern condition of our species being a case in point. The fact is that we have no grounds either for or against thinking that the emergence of language was an accident. Or, if we must think of the origins of species and of language as in some sense accidents, there is considerable ground for thinking that such accidents have happened repeatedly in the universe, and at some point of repetition accidents cease to be accidents. Darwinian biologists may bristle against the notion that the principle of language and therefore of man—whatever that "principle" might be—is contained in the extra-human ground, but a generation of space scientists have provided their spacecraft with at least rudimentary means of communication with the sentient beings of extraterrestial realms. Such simple considerations prove nothing, of course, but they may help to define the issue. The obstacles to accepting Burke's thought are very few, and they are not clearly insuperable.

It is perhaps more to the point that there is a tendency in modern thought to give up, at long last, the Cartesian dream of certainty. In the case of Richard Rorty it is Heidegger's hermeneutics that inspires this decision.[4] Another of the younger philosophers, Robert Nozick, maintains that logic cannot prevail and that the goal of philosophy is not a truly compelling reasoning: "The goal is getting to a place worth being."[5] With enthusiasm, Heidegger says that the thinking of Being can "grant us the possibility of dwelling in the world in a totally different way."[6] Less sanguine, Burke says of his "Definition of Man," a summary of Dramatism, "The best I can do is state my belief that things might be improved somewhat if enough people began thinking along the lines of this definition."[7]

A measure of the achievement of both Heidegger and Burke is that they touch with a certain inanity any effort to judge them. They have attempted reconstruction within a world constituted by language, and they require us to ask if language is a solipsism in the qualified sense which I have earlier indicated. That is the basic question. If it is a solipsism, where do we find a perspective from which to judge them? What terministic screen shall we use? Undoubtedly the perspective that prevails in academia is a residual positivism, which is the tool of an anxious predilection for judgment that is perhaps part of an occupational neurosis. Positivism, which was an extension of nineteenth-century science, finds the authority for its demand for certainty now undermined by science. The more fashionable perspectives share their origins with Heidegger and Burke in language and in Nietzsche or they have their origins in Heidegger himself. Structuralism was, of course, a kind of thinking of being.

The most exhaustive opposition to the notion of a philosophy of being is to be found, of course, in "deconstructionism" and the element of "postmodernism" for which "deconstructionism" is largely responsible. The topic will lead to the question of the philosophical relevance of Heidegger and Burke for literary theory. The careless, popular use of the term "deconstructionism" tends to veil the issue that it poses. "Deconstructionism" is most fundamentally defined as the denial of the concept of being; it is the hostile and militant polar antithesis of a philosophy of being. Furthermore, the concept of being the eradication of which is the mission of "deconstructionism" is elaborated in its most extreme possibilities. Every entity which might be conceived as mediated in experience by language, every possible "being" of any kind, is interpreted as the illusion of "presence," the illusion of being. The qualified solipsism of language found in Heidegger and Burke becomes absolute: *"There is nothing outside of the text."*[8] This means that Western civilization is unremittingly and exhaustively pervaded by the concept of being. As consequence, "deconstructionism" maintains (1) that this condition exposes Western civilization as utterly fallacious, oppressive, and corrupt, and (2) that our capacity now to understand this condition is bringing Western civilization to a close, and we are therefore at the end of a cultural epoch of some three thousand years' duration. Thus "deconstructionism" nourishes apocalypse. It is animated by undaunted faith in a deliverance the character of which it admittedly cannot describe. One might conclude that, in light of its extremism, there are only two possibilities for the future of "deconstructionism." It may ally itself with an overt program for political revolution, and if such a program becomes an effective social force, "deconstructionism," as an intellectual parasite, may be sustained by political impulse without regard for its theoretical inadequacies. The other possibility for "deconstructionism" is that without the fuel of political enthusiasm, it will continue to harden into tradition, and we may begin to take the time to read with care what its theorists have had to say. In a lengthy appendix to this study I maintain that the theories of "deconstructionism" will not bear analysis. Certain aspects of the thought of Derrida, however, are sufficiently rigorous to bring into clarity the issue posed by a philosophy of being. However much we may dislike harsh dichotomies, "deconstructionism" imposes one. It makes inescapable the conclusion that any approach to literature that is not "deconstructive" has implicit in it a philosophy of being.

It is no accident that both Heidegger and Burke have been proposed by avant-garde critics as correctives of the hermetic isolation imposed on literature by not only the New Criticism but also the "deconstructionists" in literary criticism who are the true heirs of the New Criticism, as Frank Lentricchia in *After the New Criticism* was the first to point out. In *Criticism and Social Change* Lentricchia espouses Burke's critical practice as the means whereby literature can be returned to the world to become continuous with life.[9] Paul Bové, in *Destructive Poetics: Heidegger and Modern Poetry,* has proposed the hermeneutics of Heidegger as serving that purpose.[10] It is of interest that Lentricchia and Bové adopt eventually the same political orientation. In a recent article Bové proposes as the essential "postmodernist" concern an "oppositionism" based on Stanley Aronowitz's *The Crisis in Historical Materialism: Class, Politics and Culture in Marxist Theory.*[11] Lentricchia's "Marxism" consists of this same "oppositionism."

The instinct to turn in an era of "postmodernism" to philosophers of being is perhaps inevitable. That instinct responds to needs which reach crisis in the "postmodernist" milieu. The divestment of the world of reality is the result of the entire history of post-Cartesian thought and was far advanced in the nineteenth century. In a world in which nothing seemed real, art was first endowed with autonomy and isolation, first as an alternative to reality and then as a reality alternative to the world. The Kantian aesthetic was the first and necessary step in the process; its eventual progeny, amidst the continuing attrition of the world, was "art for art's sake," which in the twentieth century found its equivalent in the New Criticism. The isolation of literature from the world in the deconstructive theory of Paul de Man has a totally different origin, the logic of default. Because in the theory of de Man—which I consider to be without foundation—every literary text deconstructs itself—self-destructs, we might say—no text can have relevance to anything. Beyond literature, the "deconstructionism" of Derrida is the belated celebration of the absence of foundations. "Deconstructionism" is a symptom. Much earlier all foundations seemed to be disappearing. Nietzsche's wasteland was growing in his time, but for so long as the environment was capable of being ordered artistically, art could provide a surrogate reality. The environment could be ordered artistically while chaos, however acute, was perceptible only philosophically, while it remained abstract and at a distance. But rather suddenly in the years following World War Two, the immediate environment seemed to go into convulsion. Nuclear death was established as a permanent menace. Populations exploded. Economic and social disorganization pervaded the globe. A senseless televised war ravaged the Western psyche. Instinct was debilitated in a sexual revolution which involved the collapse of traditional institutions. Sense and mind were overwhelmed in the omnipresent crackle of electronic "information." Ideological certainties collapsed. Corporate immensities proliferated everywhere to establish an ambient of power threatening not only the freedom and economic welfare of individuals but their very lives in a deluge of industrial waste. Everywhere dreams of decency were undermined by hopes for survival. There came into being a state of affairs, which, as Adorno says, "is everywhere producing an ego weakness which eradicates the concept of subject as individuality."[12] The corollary of this ego weakness is a radical degradation of the sense of reality, and the recoiling ego grasps at a final hope for reality in intellectual consistency.

For the arts this last hope required that criticism become philosophy. We may easily believe that the impulse to consistency so explained underlies the proliferation of critical theory in the past two decades. In the light of this need and against this background, deconstructionism plays a unique role. To a large extent it gratifies the need for intellectual consistency as a minimal occurrence of reality. It achieves this, however, by the sacrifice of a large part of reality. It can practice an impeccable consistency because of the two components of all the significant thought of the past, synthesis and analysis, it credits only analysis. Synthesis is always a gamble, always at risk. Indeed, synthesis is inevitably guilty of the deconstructionist sin of "presence," the illusion of being. As soon as deconstructionism attempts synthesis, it becomes inconsistent, a fact that I will particularize elsewhere. Because deconstructionism generally abjures synthesis, it does more than gratify the need for consistency. It becomes a fantasy of power. Analysis is necessarily dismemberment, destruction. Before the power of deconstructionism all civilization seems to cower. Deconstructionism can tolerate no concept that is not in the service of destruction. Its affirmation of "free play" and the escape into freedom from language is the grossest kind of mythologizing, a posing of conceptual possibilities for which there is not a modicum of evidence. By obviously mythical devices—mythic joys and mythic freedoms—deconstructionism attempts to resist the fact that it is the ultimate expression of what Nietzsche, its master, condemned as "resentment." The destructive program of "deconstruction," a strategic euphemism, is, on the other hand, inspired by a consistency so immaculate that it holds the promise of its own self-immolation. Deconstructionism readily acknowledges that the very language and concepts by which it achieves its destructions share fully the error and illusion, the bondage to language, of the concepts in the deconstruction of which they are employed. So eventually all must go. Deconstructionism is a phoenix which promises not to arise from its own ashes. However, deconstructionism has had the value of helping us to recognize our alternatives. The activity of criticism requires a philosophy of being if it is not to become an inanity of repeated deconstructions.

It is therefore ironic that Lentricchia and Bové have gone to philosophers of being for the foundations of their own critical programs but have done so only on the condition of revising those philosophers in such a way as to eliminate the concept of being, thus accommodating their masters to that aspect of postmodernism for which deconstructionism is chiefly responsible. In Bové's *Destructive Poetics* Heidegger becomes a deconstructionist. Bové draws upon Heidegger's hermeneutic, as developed in *Being and Time,* to call for "destructive" criticism, and, what is more, for "destructive" poetry. This painfully distorts Heidegger, as does all "postmodernist" exploitation of Heidegger. Bové reports the hermeneutic reliably but falsifies it by emphasis and application. According to Heidegger, the "fore-structure" that is projected upon the future in every interpretation is constituted by the past, and interpretation is a circle, but the repetition it involves is not a simple repetition of the past. The problem confronted by every authentic interpretation is that the insights of the past are rendered inauthentic as tradition is contaminated by the "idle talk," "gossip," and "curiosity" of the "they-world." Bové's first problem is that he must see poetry as rendered inauthentic by this process. This ignores the fact that *Being and Time,* which Heidegger considered incomplete at the time of publication, does not deal with poetry at all and that all subsequent references to poetry are patently incompatible with the notion that poetry of the past has become inauthentic. Bové's emphasis also distorts. He correctly acknowledges the positive element of interpretation, quoting the following from Heidegger: "In proposing our 'definition' of 'truth' we have not *shaken off* the tradition, but we have *appropriated* it primordially."[13] Nevertheless, Bové must say, "*Being and Time* establishes destruction as *the* hermeneutic stance of the authentic logos." Heidegger uses the word "destruction" repeatedly but his emphasis is very different from Bové's: "But to bury the past in nullity . . . is not the purpose of this destruction; its aim is *positive*; its negative function remains unexpressed and indirect." Heidegger says that the "repetition" of interpretation is "the *repetition* of a possibility of existence that has come down to us." He says, "The authentic repetition of a possibility of existence that has been" is "the possibility that Dasein may choose its hero." Bové's em-

phasis is always as follows: "Heidegger's destruction, i.e., his interpretation . . . ." The negative emphasis results in a "poetics" which
places its prime value on a kind of poetry which is "in the service of
disclosing nothingness."[14] The shift of emphasis becomes a shift of
meaning. Bové resorts to Derrida's vocabulary throughout, and inevitably the "nothing" that was for Heidegger an inalienable element of
being becomes the "nothing" in which Derrida abolishes being. The
interpretative process, says Bové, "leads the authentic critic back in
his own history of interpretations—which, of course, are themselves
destructive interpretations as all authentic histories must be—to a
Nothing." Bové's "poetics" draws finally into complete accord with
Derrida: "Ultimately, then, there emerges a theory of literature which
sees all language as based on nothing and manifests itself as fiction
emerging out of and reflecting nothing." The hermeneutic of Heidegger, which is always interpretation of being, ends up as "postmodernist" nihilism: "Authentic critical interpretation confronts this constant destructive shifting among truths and errors with no hope at all
of making sense of it all."[15] Bové's work simply repeats the adaptation
of Heidegger which constitutes the thought of Derrida, going Derrida one better in the more emphatic word "destructive." Bové is apparently oblivious of the fact that a criticism with "no hope at all of
making sense of it all" returns literature to the hermetic isolation
from which his version of Heidegger was supposed to release it. If
Bové intended his work as what Heidegger called a "retrieve"—a
reading of what a philosopher did not but should have thought—he
should have said so, acknowledging that he has rejected the fundamental thought of the man to whose authority he appeals.

Similarly, Lentricchia appropriates Burke for his critical program,
but, as we have seen, interprets Burke as "deconstructing" the concept of the act, thus divesting Burke of the thought essential to the
philosophy of being which underlies everything Burke has written.
Lentricchia has done a real service for our understanding of Burke by
relating aspects of Burke's thought to the thought of Antonio Gramsci. Burke's political thought, says Lentricchia, is "remarkably close to
Gramsci's revision of the vulgarities of economism." Lentricchia has
formulated a Neo-Marxist position for which he takes the thought of
Burke as the necessary point of departure: Burke's thought is "the re-
pository of principles without which what I think of as healthy criticism cannot function." The effect of Lentricchia's reading is to op-
timize what he correctly calls Burke's "uncanny contemporaneity."[16]

That, I think, is an invaluable service to Burke, who is a difficult writer, and it can be a boon to humanistic studies. On the other hand, Burke's thought is diminished by his being mustered into the partisan service of Marxism, however mild and benign a Marxism it may be. Burke's revision of Marxism is only part of his vast revision and assimilation of modern knowledge. It is a revision in which elements of Marxism become part of Burke as they have become a part of most modern thought. Burke shares some basic Marxist values—what civilized human being does not?—but it has never been possible to label Burke a Marxist. Indeed, Lentricchia requires that label only because he chooses it. In this there is a sense in which Lentricchia, who rejects "deconstructionism" as literary theory, has opted for a philosophy of being. Marxism is, finally, a philosophy of being. It is significant that the meanings of the terms "dialectical materialism" and "historical materialism" are comprehended by the conception of "the paradox of substance." More importantly where Lentricchia is concerned, his Neo-Marxism, as he makes clear, is an option against philosophy and for action, even though that action is to be an oppositionism coherent with academic order. The option for action is an act of faith, and the thought of being is implicit in every act of faith. Few have done more than Derrida to make that clear.

The very distortions by which Bové and Lentricchia have appropriated Heidegger and Burke bear witness to the urgency of the need for the thought of these men. The two bodies of thought are, in a way that I believe to be essential, complementary. Bové is correct in seeing the configuration of Heidegger's hermeneutic as the aspect of his thought that is most important for criticism. The hermeneutic projection is always a human act, and Heidegger and Burke meet in this conception. However, Heidegger's configuration provides a temporal definition of the act that is lacking in Burke's thought. Burke's conception of the act within the pentad is a synchronic display which, although it is open to time and history, is not articulated in a diachronic dimension. Heidegger's hermeneutic may be applied as an enrichment of Burke's concept of the act and the pentad. However, if the complementarity of the two writers is to result in synthesis, it may do so only by requiring a revision, not of Burke, but of Heidegger. The reconciling revision would frankly modify Heidegger's conception and it would do so radically, but it would not reverse its import as has occurred in Bové's treatment.

Fundamentally Heidegger's thought resists the integration of art in life that occurs in Burke. The wording of "The Origin of the Work of Art" sustains the autonomy of the work of art: "The establishing of truth in the work is the bringing forth of a being such as never was before and will never come to be again." Heidegger says, "To submit to this displacement [that occurs in the work of art] means to transform our accustomed ties to world and to earth and henceforth to restrain all usual doing and prizing, knowing and looking, in order to stay within the truth that is happening in the work."[17] Clearly art is not another instance of the acts which constitute life in general. The absolute uniqueness of the work of art, its transforming "our accustomed ties to the world and earth," and our restraining "all accustomed ties to world and to earth" are to be explained by the "ontological difference," the difference between beings and Being, between two distinct realms, the ontic and the ontological. This is the basic premise of Heidegger's thought, early and late. It means that the effort to think, or describe Being, occurs at a level of "reality" from which the rest of knowledge is derivative and to the analysis or description of which it is irrelevant. This is also the level of reality at which poetry exists, as Heidegger's constant resort to poetry in the thinking of Being, especially the poetry of Hölderlin, makes clear. Heidegger may be seen as returning poetry to life only if we accept the ontological difference. To accept that is to accept the thought of Heidegger without qualification. For Heidegger, "thinking"—which is always "the thinking of Being"—and poetry share the same neighborhood. It is very near to the neighborhood of the New Criticism and the Kantian aesthetic and in the same exclusive area of the city.

For Burke, art is an instance of the rhetorical activity which is ceaseless in life, and being happens within and as part of the multifariousness of life. The pentad is the paradigm of that happening, a paradigm of being as human act, which is also a paradigm of art, and a plan for criticism in which all knowledge becomes at least potentially of use: "The main ideal of criticism, as I conceive it, is to use all that is there to use."[18] A perspective opens in which any critical concept, except positivism and deconstructionism, may take on primary usefulness. Criticism opens to all the elements of modern critical theory such as those anticipated by Burke: a revised Marxism, a revised Freudianism, hermeneutics, structuralism, semiotics, reader-response theory, theory of ritual, speech-act theory, and even, as we have seen, a qualified kind of deconstructionism. The wide range of philosophical concepts that Burke has discovered to be not rigorous and necessary logical constructs, but "poetic action," continue to constitute a part of the knowledge of the past which may be fruitfully projected as future in the creative act. Virtually all knowledge may be of use, but no concept may be employed except under the recognition of the limitations of its inherent finitude and its role within a context. Every combination of concepts which may be generated by the variegated stimulus of the pentad must resign itself to inconclusiveness, recognizing that the act as nucleus of life may be penetrated by analysis only as deadly falsification.

In the centrality of the act, for Burke there is implicit the aesthetic emphasis in his thought, an emphasis which consists in a persistent taking of delight in the complexities of all things as they have been and as they are. The "postmodernist" bias that disparages this aspect of Burke's thought is wrong, but there is no doubt that this aspect of his thought exists. I think that it is essential to Burke and of unquestionable value. Its role in Burke's thought, I am convinced, must be its role in education, which must remain fundamentally an aesthetic enterprise. The point is that values are either supernatural, or political, or aesthetic, or they are hygenic, which means that they are necessities and not values. To orient education politically, as some writers are now proposing, would be to limit and to vitiate education. Inevitably to propose that education must be essentially aesthetic is to awaken hard-fixed postmodernist bugaboos. But education conceived as primarily aesthetic does not conjure the obscure liberalism of "liberal education" and it does not demand the futilities of "interdisciplinary study" as a value in itself. It does not evoke Matthew Arnold's fuzzy conception of "culture," and if it makes education an end in itself, as all pleasures are ends in themselves, its purpose is certainly not to make "the gentleman," or "the lady." Above all, it does not propose a lush relaxation in hedonistic joy. It simply recognizes as the highest value governing education the kind of pleasure which the human organism by intense development within the complexities of civilization may enjoy. It does mean that literature—to postmodernist abhorrence—will become again an object of pleasure as are mathematics and philosophy. Education must remain separate from praxis if it is not to repress permanently the possibilities of praxis. This does not mean that education can be objective. It means that it remains open to the extent that its criteria are aesthetic, finding all apt designs, all good arguments, pleasurable. To conceive education as aesthetic is to recognize that every animal plays before it works or fights.

For Burke the aesthetic is prior to the political and eventually determines it, and the aesthetic is neither frivolous, nor capricious, nor exclusive. We are beyond the Kantian aesthetic. For Burke the aesthetic is a factor of the needs of the human organism—its needs being always needs for pleasure—in relationship to the threats of the environment. This is why he has argued that aesthetics should be derived, not from the beautiful, but from the sublime: "the *threat* is the basis of beauty." Burke provides the grounds for aesthetic analysis in a passage in which he denies the unity of the subject. The individual, says, Burke, is made up of "sub-identities, subpersonalities, 'voices'." These "subpersonalities" constitute the condition addressed by the creative act: "the poet seeks to build the symbolic superstructures that put them together into a comprehensive 'super-personality'." [19] Here, as at almost every turn, Burke's reception is imperiled by a gamut of entrenched preconceptions which will distort his thought. Such passages inspire "postmodernist" protests that Burke remains in the grip of Romanticism, which requires the unity of art and interprets it as an expression of the personality, both the unity and the personality being sanctioned by a metaphysics of cosmic organicism. The key words are "the poet seeks to build"; he does not *become* a "super-personality." The "sub-identities," the "voices," have origins external to the individual and their unity is sanctioned only by, and consists only in, the "symbolic superstructure," the character of which is exhausted by rhetorical analysis. The only organism involved, the only "subject," is the human body. Burke says, "The natural tendency of symbolic enterprise is towards integration." He means that the tendency has its origin in the human organism, the constant unifying activity of which is the most basic of biological facts. For Burke the human organism is always the ultimate reference. A "deconstructionism" that conceives language as separate from the organism and a Marxism that discounts the aesthetic are true Gnosticisms. The body in negotiation with the culture is the energy of the act that engenders being.

Burke's thought comprehends most of the elements of "postmodernism," though in Burke these elements are always devoid of the absolutism—that going to the end of the line—that is a "postmodernist" fetish. For Burke, there is no unitary subject, but there is unquestionably an organism, whose tendency is to unify. The text remains a text, protean in character, but it is not infinitely interpretable.

Language is perhaps the most decisive reality, but it is not the only reality: objects are signs and also the referents of signs. While history is of fundamental importance, human acts are among its originary components, and within history we confront choices. While education is consistent with political partisanship, it must not be controlled politically. The oppositionism so dear to "postmodernism" is an inevitable result of understanding and must not become the criterion of understanding. Criticism is, like art, a creative act, but it is not the equivalent of art and does not aspire to compete with or to supplant it. What Burke's thought rejects in "postmodernism" is its dogmatism.

Unquestionably, however, "postmodernism" enjoys itself, and some of the bases for its resistance to synthesis are worth considering. The thought of synthesis dampens the special joys of factionalism, of elitism, of the zeal of partisanship, the self-confidence of dogma, the Gnostic passions. Factionalism is also a convenience, propitious for the educational quick fix. A single orientation may be mastered easily and quickly, and in a condition where controversy is rampant, any limited perspective may claim polemic authority, which may be taken as "professional" competence. The challenge posed by Burke to academia is intimidating. Even when we have eliminated from contemporary critical theory its spurious and duplicitous polemicisms, the range of learning it demands is very great. The development of contemporary critical theory, even though it has been fully anticipated by a single thinker, is a great collective achievement. Burke's dramatism, his philosophy of being, offers the basis, perhaps the only conceivable basis, for synthesis. Synthesis in Burke will not pose the threat of stasis, which is a legitimate "postmodernist" fear. Education will sustain continuities with the past, but it will continue to participate in the transformations that most of us feel ourselves to be a part of. Indeed, there will be "totalizations"—tentative necessities of thought—but there is no threat of "closure," because Burke, like Nietzsche, finds paradox at the heart of things.

appendix

Note Against Deconstructionism

Jacques Derrida

IN Of Grammatology Jacques Derrida most fully develops his theoretical position. The theory is derived from a hypothesis that cannot be taken seriously. At the point of decisive articulation of the theory, material entirely alien to and contradictory to the theory becomes essential to it. The deficiencies of Derrida's system, or antisystem, have been surmised by many. I wish to examine the antisystem closely. To begin with, a distinction is necessary. We can imagine a "deconstructive" procedure that simply looked for and failed to find an empirical basis for the concept in question. Such a procedure has been part of a continuing tradition for nearly three centuries, beginning with Locke's criticism of "substance" and Hume's criticism of "cause," continuing, for instance, in the work of Jeremy Bentham and John Stuart Mill, and culminating in Nietzsche's nihilistic strategies. Derrida's analyses of particular concepts in particular texts are basically a continuation of this tradition and reveal no great surprises. Few can have doubted that there is something wrong with Saussure's conception of the sign as containing the concept, of which it must in some sense *be* the sign. It is hardly news that there is something wrong with Rousseau's conception of nature or that Plato's work is riddled with conceptions that are not viable in the twentieth century. Though such "deconstructions" are sometimes achievements, of at least a limited sort, they cannot be taken as in themselves supporting a theory that pretends to describe the exclusively legitimate program of Western thought, and Derrida pretends to nothing less.

"Deconstructionism," the theory called "grammatology," is the doctrine of an antigrammar so extravagant that it cannot be accepted at all without becoming dogma. The theory, exploiting apocalyptic fears instilled by universal social disorganization and permanent military crisis that poses global death, tells us that Western civilization has come to an end, not through political, social, or scientific developments, and not as the result of a degenerative process of any kind, but simply by recognition of characteristics that have maintained in Western civilization until now.[1] In effect, it is *Of Grammatology* that brings Western civilization to an end. We are told, furthermore, that "grammatology" is the product of historical necessity.[2] Derrida appears in robes of prophecy gifted with a vision into the "distance of a few centuries."[3] It must be understood that one cannot accept "grammatology" without recognizing it as a "truth" that supplants all the "truths" of the past. Indeed, we are told, in italics, that "*in a certain sense 'thought' means nothing,*" and *Of Grammatology* pretends to make it clear that "thinking is what we already know we have not yet begun."[4] "Grammatology" is a theoretical construct in which there is implicit beforehand the deconstruction of the world. And not only does grammatology make "deconstruction" necessary; with all the thought of the past in ruins, "deconstruction" becomes the only legitimate, indeed, the only possible intellectual enterprise—except for something called "writing," which is licensed by "deconstructionism" and which will be examined below. What I here attribute to "deconstructionism" must certainly seem exaggerated. If so, it is because we hesitate, courteously, to believe that Derrida means what he says. The fact is that until "deconstructionism" two millennia had not brought us a dogma of such purport. Claims of such magnitude have a poetic power that tends to suspend our powers of disbelief.

While Derrida is obviously too bright to have any doubt about what he is up to, most of his readers have failed to recognize the fundamentally mythic, fictional character of all the intellectual tools that are peculiarly Derrida's own and that constitute the thus mythic foundation of his theoretical position. That his readers have failed to recognize this is to be explained chiefly by two circumstances. First, Derrida's prose is designed as a strategy of obfuscation. Second, he has exploited a universal ignorance about the nature of language. Our growing awareness of the profound importance of language combined with the fact that we have no basic understanding of language makes it seem that anything is possible.

We should begin, however, by outlining some of the things that most people might take for granted as fairly obvious characteristics of language. We assume first of all that many of the things we talk about do actually have existence independently of language and that we do actually and quite often talk about something other than language. We assume that what exists includes a great deal more than language and that we are aware of a very large extension of the world that is not constituted by language. Even if we assume that language is effective in all perception and in one way or another shapes all objects of perception, we are also convinced that external objects are immediately and decisively distinguishable from the language in which we talk about them. So we continue to assume that language is referential. Most of us make such assumptions as the following: Within memory, links are developed between certain images and certain patterns of sound, with the result that experiences of images will evoke memories of words in a process essential to the possibility of speaking. Furthermore, in the opinion of a great many people including most modern psychologists, the sound patterns of words are capable, in one degree or another, of evoking image memories. The carefully ordered language of narrative and poetry seems capable of eliciting images with some fullness and power. Such images are very different in intensity from the images that arise with hallucinatory power in psychosis, in dream, and in response to drugs and to electrode stimulus of the neocortex, but it would seem probable that the memory sources of images are the same in both cases. Freud, in *The Interpretation of Dreams*, provides a convincing explanation of the fact that the ordinary recall of images does not achieve hallucinatory power. It has also occurred to most people that language is saturated with affectivity and that, if only in this sense, language always has meaning. We would conclude then that language is always implicated in the neuronal system, in muscle tone, in affect. Language functions in intimate relation to the human organism, and the slightest reflection suggests that language has no existence that is free of that relationship.

One measure of the extremity of "deconstructionism" is that it emphatically excludes all the apparently innocent assumptions about language that have been outlined above. We may best approach Derrida's theoretical position by outlining the moves by which he effects this radical exclusion. They are as follows: (1) interpreting in what I will call an absolutist way the concept of being which he rejects; (2) conceiving in an absolutist way the nature of "the subject" which he rejects; (3) treating language as a closed system, as isolate and autonomous, and its dynamisms as strictly formal and internal; (4) retreating at a crucial point in his argument into the solipsism of the Husserlian reduction.

The fundamental characteristic of the Western civilization that is said to be coming to an end, and by virtue of which it is ending, is "logocentrism," or what Derrida, following Heidegger, also calls "metaphysics." The abiding and exhaustively pervasive error of logocentrism is that it fosters the concept of being. Derrida's absolutist version of "being" is what he calls "presence." The real enormity of what we are dealing with consists in the fact that presence, which is always an error, occurs in every substantive concept known to Western discourse prior to Derrida. Derrida gives us a list of the following concepts in which presence occurs: "the thing" as present "to the sight as eidos," that is, as image; "substance/essence/existence"; "temporal presence" as the moment of the present; "the cogito, consciousness, subjectivity" as "self-presence"; "the co-presence of the other and of the self"; "intersubjectivity as the intentional phenomenon of the ego, and so forth." Elsewhere Derrida says, "It could be shown that all the names related to fundamentals, to principles, or to the center have always designated an invariable presence." Eventually, the error of presence occurs in every word which we assume to be referential: "The formal essence of the signified is presence." Derrida says, "to make enigmatic what one thinks one understands by the words 'proximity', 'immediacy', 'presence' . . . is my final intention in this book. This deconstruction of presence accomplishes itself through the deconstruction of consciousness," that is, of the subject. Much of modern thought involves an anti-Cartesian rejection of consciousness conceived as a unitary subject. For Derrida, rejection of the subject means rejection of the organism. His theory occupies a realm "'anterior' to all *physiological* problematics concerning the nature of the *engramme*," or the physiological coding of memory. (The *engramme* is an outmoded conception.) And, as Derrida says, the absence of the subject is "also the absence of the thing or the referent." So the consideration of language as Derrida conceives it excludes both biology and psychology. He hardly needs to say, "Psychology will never be able to accommodate within its space that which constitutes the absence of the signatory [subject], to say nothing of the absence of the referent."[5] The case is graver still. Rather obviously, with the removal of the subject and the object, there remains for Derrida nothing but language. The "axial proposition" of his essay, he says, is, *"There is nothing outside of the text."*[6] When language is all that is left, there is nothing left to consider but its formal, internal dynamisms. I will postpone for a while consideration of Derrida's retreat into the transcendental realm of the Husserlian reduction.

"There is nothing outside of the text" (Derrida's italics). It will be best to begin with what that cannot mean. It cannot mean what Heidegger means when he says that language is both the "lighting" and "concealing" of being. It cannot mean what Burke means when he says that language is a "reflection," a "selection," and a "deflection" of reality. For Heidegger and for Burke, that which exists within language also extends beyond it; it is "outside of the text." It is something separate from language that language brings into experience and to which language also refers. For Derrida, however, the signified "is *always already in the position of the signifier.*" In itself, this seems ambiguous, but we may be sure that it means that we can not distinguish the signified from the signifier, for Derrida says, "To this epoch [the epoch of logocentrism, or all of Western history] belongs the difference between the signified and the signifier."[7] For grammatology, then, this difference does not exist. We are forced to the conclusion that the "axial proposition" of *Of Grammatology* means: there is nothing but language; only language exists. In Derrida linguistic solipsism is absolute. Language is a circle hermetically closed, and it is the world.

Obviously the conception has at least some merits. It is true that much of modern language theory moves in this direction. From Charles Sanders Peirce, Derrida has justification for the statement *"The thing itself is a sign."*[8] Kenneth Burke has said as much. Following Heidegger and Burke, we may argue that we never know anything except as it is revealed by language and except as it takes its character from language. We can never get outside of language in order to examine the existent "in itself." This does not carry us to a total solipsism. To say that the thing, the signified, is a sign does not bring us to the conclusion that the signified is a kind of sign which cannot be distinguished from the kind of sign that is the signifier. So far, that conclusion would depend on a purely verbal logic. It is probably true, nevertheless, that we are tempted to the final conclusion—there is no signified—because in the tendency to linguistic solipsism there is a parallel with Berkeley's solipsism. However, the solipsistic argument from language is utterly distinct from Berkeley's argument, which is that we can never establish the objects of sense impressions because we could do so only on the basis of other sense impressions. The argument from language cannot establish total solipsism because the argument occurs this side of Berkeley's argument. Insofar as the issue of the existence of a signified is concerned, the argument from language does not begin with this question: Do existents objectively exist? The pertinent question is, Do we have in fact sense responses that are not totally a product of language, and is language related referentially to such responses? Dr. Johnson's kicking the stone does not refute Berkeley, as Dr. Johnson thought, but it is quite sufficient to refute total solipsism based on the argument from language. For Derrida, however, it would be unacceptable to think of the sign as a sound pattern which has a sense impression, or the memory of a sense impression, as its referent. The sense impression or the memory of it would thus become "presence."

The distinction is of the greatest importance for understanding the nature of Derrida's solipsism. Derrida has said that the sign must be deconstructed, and by that he means the sign as conceived by Saussure, who is one of the most important sources of Derrida's thought. For Saussure the sign is a combination of a "sound-image" and a "concept." But for "sound-image" or sound-pattern, Saussure substitutes "signifier," and for "concept," he substitutes "signified." In a language made up of signs which contain that which is signified we come at least to the verge of the linguistic solipsism that is so obvious in Derrida. But another point must be made about Saussure's "sign." Saussure's combination of the signifier and the signified in the sign reflects an awareness that the signifier, the sound-image, and the concept cannot be separated. This means that one way of "deconstructing" Saussure's sign would be to discover that the *"signifier" is* the "concept," in accord with the theories of the psychologist Lev Vygotsky and the neuropsychologist A. R. Luria. It is difficult to escape that conclusion when Derrida says, "We *think only in signs.*"[9] This, however, would leave open the possibility that sound-patterns-concepts are linked with and refer to sense impressions or memories of sense-impressions, but as has been pointed out, this would mean that grammatology would open to "presence" and with that the theory, the dogma, of "deconstructionism" would collapse. We will better understand Derrida's absolutist conception of "presence" when we realize that what he presents solemnly as theory in *Of Grammatology* is derived from his deconstructive method, which is admittedly only a polemical device based on a fiction.

The point of departure for Derrida's method is apparently Nietzsche's comment that "the false opposites in which the people, and *consequently* language, believe, have always been dangerous hindrances to the advance of truth." [10] What Derrida deconstructs are "hierarchical oppositions" the first terms of which are "repressive" of the second— oppositions such as "nature/culture," "meaning/form," "outside/inside." In the analysis of *Of Grammatology* we are most interested in the oppositions "speech/writing," "signified/signifier," "identity/difference," "presence/absence." "In a classical philosophical opposition," says Derrida, "we are not dealing with the peaceful coexistence of a vis-à-vis, but rather with a violent hierarchy. One of the two terms governs the other (axiologically, logically, etc.), or has the upper hand. To destruct the opposition, first of all, is to overturn the hierarchy at a given moment." [11] Now the purpose of the overturned, or reversed, hierarchy, the reversed opposition, is not to establish a reality, a truth, but to achieve "a general *displacement* of the system," that is, the system of the original opposition and eventually the entire system which is logocentrism. [12] Derrida does not pretend that the reversed opposition has any more authority than the original opposition. The reversed opposition by virtue of being an opposition remains *within* logocentrism, as Derrida readily admits. Oppositions are a basic fallacy of logocentrism. So the reversed oppositions, like the original oppositions, are mythic constructs. *Of Grammatology* takes its character fundamentally from the fact that the basic conceptions constituting its theory are derived from the reversal of hierarchical oppositions. In other words, Derrida's theory, grammatology, is designed to make a program and an obligation of Derrida's deconstructions, which consist in the application of his method. It turns out, however, that the basic premise of the theory is in fact the method itself, which is only a polemical device. In the description of Derrida's method in *Positions*, the key move is "to overturn the hierarchy at a given moment." Derrida is laconic about that "given moment," and we will want to keep an eye on it. At this moment Derrida will "determine" something which the history that is philosophy "has been able to dissimulate or forbid, making itself into a history by means of this somewhere motivated repression."[13] For Derrida Western philosophy is a conspiracy that he will unmask, but it is extremely difficult to credit the candor of his own claims. Derrida tells us unabashedly that at the moment of this revelation, he will work "from a certain exterior that is unqualifiable or unnamable by philosophy."[14] Five lines later Derrida makes it clear that the philosophy that cannot qualify or name this "exterior" is "the West." So deconstructionism is both apocalyptic and a mysterious operation; we are unable to say that it is not magical.

Though Derrida is deeply indebted to Saussure, a large part of *Of Grammatology* is directed against Saussure's conception of the spoken language, rather than writing, as the proper study of linguistics.[15] The hierarchical opposition which Derrida will reverse is "speech/writing." The priority given to speech, Derrida says, results from an illusion. The phenomenon of hearing oneself speak creates the illusion that language, in speech, is in immediate contact with thought, with its signified, with "presence."[16] By comparison, writing seems a degradation, an alienation, in which possibilities of falsification of thought are multiplied. It is this ancient illusion which produces the repressive "speech/writing." It must be understood that this is the fundamental hierarchical opposition. It is the key to the error of the West, the abiding error falsifying an entire civilization, the error that is logocentrism: "The system of language associated with phonetic-alphabetic writing is that within which logocentric metaphysics, determining the sense of being as presence, has been produced."[17]

Derrida maintains first that there is no essential difference between speech and writing; there is no opposition. The identity of speech and writing consists in their sharing the essential character which they take from "difference" and "absence."[18] We will return later to difference. But if there is no opposition, how are we to "practice a *reversal* of the classical opposition" and effect "a general displacement of the system"? This is to be achieved on the basis of something else that speech and writing have in common: they are derived from the same thing, something that is antecedent to writing and speech. We come now to that "particular moment." Derrida now declares the existence of a prelinguistic articulation which he calls "arche-writing." Assuming that such exists, we may observe that it might as easily have been called "arche-speech," and with somewhat more probability, but that, as we will see, would have destroyed the game. And we confront a deeper problem. For the moment let us say "arche-writing." But where does it come from? What is the evidence for it? There is no evidence whatever: it "cannot and can never be recognized as the *object of a science.*"[19] But we know where it comes from. It is a new name for the prelinguistic articulation which Heidegger in *Being and Time* called "Discourse" (*Rede*, which means speech), a conception which Heidegger later abandoned. It is also clear why Derrida needed to lift this concept from a superseded text. Derrida's deconstructive method simply required it. Without it, he cannot reverse the hierarchical opposition "speech/writing." The reversal becomes possible because Derrida chooses to call his prelinguistic articulation both "arche-writing" and "writing" because, he says, arche-writing "essentially communicates with the vulgar concept of writing."[20] When "arche-writing" becomes "writing," giving us two names for the same thing, this permits, or seems to permit, the new reversed hierarchical opposition—"writing/speech." "Yet writing had to appear even before there was a question of speech."[21] A further consequence is that hereafter Derrida will use the word "writing" in two entirely different senses, though usually when he says "writing" he means "arche-writing."

With the myth of "writing" now planted, the myth can grow. "Arche-writing" is true "writing," which is betrayed and falsified by both speech and writing as "logocentrism." And the myth continues. "Writing" is antecedent to "vulgar" writing and speech, and "writing itself" is the "origin of language."[22] But more than that: it is possible to recoup "writing," to return to "writing." Derrida assures us that this is not a return to innocence, which would reflect the kind of nostalgia for which he berates Lévi-Strauss. But if truly "pure" writing is only a working hypothesis, there is no doubt for Derrida that our age is one of "suspense between two ages of writing" and "we are beginning to write, to write differently."[23] So certain privileged people can actually do "arche-writing" which is "writing" and escape from logocentrism. As we have seen, Heidegger, by drawing a line through "Being," achieves the first "writing," and it is presumably what we hear in the occasional mumbling of the discourse of the later Heidegger. Grammatology, Derrida tells us, is a concept of "plurivocity," and grammatology is "possible" on "the condition of knowing what writing is." Writing is "pluri-dimensional symbolic thought." Derrida tells us that modern poetry as represented by Mallarmé and the poetics of Ezra Pound was "the first break in the most entrenched Western tradition."[24] It must be obvious, however, that logocentrism and metaphysics, as Derrida and Heidegger conceived them, are breached by all real poetry of all times, as Heidegger's own recourse to the poetry of the past makes clear. Nevertheless, we may understand that some of Derrida's essays are virtually unintelligible because they are efforts to recoup "arche-writing."

All possible arguments for "arche-writing" are empty deductions designed to serve Derrida's method by a theory that will justify it, but like all good readers of Derrida we may search for persuasive grounds for what he says. We are told that "writing," or "arche-writing," is "the origin of language," and it is when Derrida attempts to explain the link between "arche-writing" and language that we will most clearly see the duplicity of his thought. For the moment, it is important to reflect that such a link is exceedingly hard to imagine. It would not do to maintain that without an articulation temporally prior to language there would have been no basis for the articulation which is language, for then "arche-writing" would constitute a kind of knowledge of which language would be a representation, though a bad representation, and "arche-writing" would thus become the referent of language; accordingly Derrida has not proposed such an explanation. If "arche-writing" is in any way prior to language, we are inevitably puzzled as to how it could be characterized by "plurivocity" or have anything in common with "pluri-dimensional thought." As victims of logocentrism and therefore of historical and evolutionary ideas, we might try to imagine a prelinguistic animal condition in which "arche-writing" prevailed. One might then hesitate to credit the value of recouping "arche-writing." If we imagined, as many do, that language is characterized by referentiality that developed gradually from non-referential animal sounds, then there would have been no articulation prior to language, for all animal responses would have been instinctual, which would mean that animals respond to a limited number of distinct and isolated stimuli and that all the other potential stimuli of the environment would have no existence at all for the prelinguistic animal. Of course, we have been forbidden the conception of referentiality. Furthermore, all historical and evolutionary considerations must be taken as in bad taste, for all Derrida's theoretical conceptions belong to an ideal realm from which history, biology, psychology, and anthropology have been excluded.

We come then to recognize the extreme difficulty posed for us by grammatology. All that we already know, all substantive science, is excluded from our understanding of language. It is most provocative to observe in this connection that grammatology in being prior to all other knowledge becomes a negative version of the ontology of Heidegger which is prior to all other knowledge. The problem of understanding grammatology is also that what constitutes the theory, the basic theoretical vocabulary, consists of terms which Derrida calls "undecidables." That in itself might be taken to forestall inquiry. However, what we want to know is not so much what the "undecidables" are, how they are decided, but how they came to be. It should be kept in mind that only if nothing exists except language can we make any sense at all of the undecidables.

The truly basic "undecidable" is "trace." To become acquainted with—though not of course to comprehend—"trace," we must understand that the meaning of a word does not derive from its reference to something in the world and external to language, which would be a signified. According to Derrida's theory, the meaning of the word "congressman" in the United States is not the effect of the fact that we use it to refer to a person elected to the lower house of Congress, such a person thus becoming a signified. The meaning of the word depends upon the fact that we also have the word "senator." The "meanings" of all words are derived entirely from such differences. For the sake of brevity, I quote Jonathan Culler's summary definition: "The sound sequence bat is a signifier because it contrasts with pat, mat, bad, bet, etc. That noise that is 'present' when one says *bat* is inhabited by the traces of forms one is not uttering, and it can function as a signifier only insofar as it consists of such traces." This is part of the truth about the meanings of words; taken as the whole truth, it means that there is no signified. Derrida says "the signified is originarily and essentially . . . trace" and it is "*always already in the position of the signifier.*" We will see that while Culler's definition is surely the best one can achieve, it makes "trace" much clearer than Derrida wants it to be. He says, "The trace is *nothing*, it is not an entity, it exceeds the question *What is?*" It precedes that question and "contingently makes it possible." Furthermore, "no *concept of metaphysics can describe it.*" This means that no concept available within Western thought can describe it, and one is inevitably curious as to how Derrida has conceived of it. In the question of reference as concerned in "trace," one must speak of what is absent: "The absence of *another* here-and-now, of another transcendental present, of *another* origin of the world appearing as such, presenting itself as irreducible absence within the presence of the trace, is not a metaphysical formula substituted for a scientific concept of writing."[25] This typical

Derrida sentence should be considered step by step. In what we have always thought of as "reference," one of the things that are absent is *"another* here and now"; that is, the only "here and now" that is present is "trace." Also absent is "another transcendental present." An object of reference would be transcendental in standing outside language, but the object is not present at all; "the trace," as we will see, is a transcendental, but the "trace" is present, and only the "trace." Also absent, most significantly, is *"another* origin of the world appearing as such." We can be sure that the only origin of the world is language and its product, the "trace." The object, the material existent, standing outside language, would be *"another* origin of the world," and its "appearing as such" does not occur; it is absent. The next part of the sentence is most difficult: "presenting itself as irreducible absence within the presence of the trace." Strictly speaking the "trace" is not "presence"—there is no "presence"—but if the object of reference were present it could only present "itself as irreducible absence within the presence of the trace" if the "trace" were present. All this, we are told, "is not a metaphysical formula substituted for a scientific concept of writing." I think we must grant that in some sense this escapes from "metaphysics," from "logocentrism," but Derrida also means that it is not to be taken for a "scientific concept" having an origin external to grammatology. Derrida has excluded both the physical and the social sciences.

As we have seen, "difference" and "trace" are interdependent: "difference cannot be thought without the trace." Derrida quotes Saussure, "'in language there are only differences'." In *Positions* Derrida says, "There are only everywhere, differences and traces of traces." "Difference" may be taken as Derrida's basic concept, the concept from which arises the entire miasma of his conceptual world. But "difference," prior to *Of Grammatology,* has been complicated in the creation of another "undecidable." The term is "differance," a word Derrida has invented, spelling it with an *a* with the intention of capturing the two meanings of the word *différer,* which are "to differ" and "to defer." So the sign consists of a play of differences and it is also "a deferred presence," perpetually, permanently deferred. In the essay "Differance," Derrida tells us bluntly, *"Differance* is neither a *word* nor a *concept."* When we think that presence occurs, it is really differance: "Presence is a determination and effect within a system which is no longer that of presence but that of differance." "Differance" is closely related to "trace," and "The trace cannot be conceived—nor, therefore, can differance—on the basis of either the present or the presence of the present." And "Not only is there no realm of differance, but differance is even the subversion of every realm." "Differance," Derrida tells us, inspires us with fear. Its lacking a realm "is obviously what makes it threatening and necessarily dreaded by everything in us that desires a realm." It turns out, in *Of Grammatology*—and we will want to remember this point—that the "undecidables" all mean the same thing: "*The (pure) trace is differance.*" "Writing is the other name of this differance."[26]

The audacity and persistence of Derrida's mystifications cultivate the impression that he knows something he is not telling us about or suggest that he has in fact conceived of what is incommunicable, which would mean that he has conceived the inconceivable unless we granted to him a power of intuition that his own thought rejects. Understandably his theory requires the support of philosophical authority and linguistic authority, and when we observe his effort to incorporate his philosophical sources for the support of his theoretical constructs, the prophet and mystagogue becomes very human. The fact is that he remains unusually close to his sources and in large part his theory, or antitheory, is a paste-up of what he has extracted from his sources, usually after first having "deconstructed' them. We are obviously and continuously in the company of Nietzsche, Saussure, and Heidegger. Hegel is saluted, as, in effect, Derrida's master. Hegel is "the thinker of irreducible difference"; he "rehabilitated thought as the *memory productive* of signs"; he is the "first thinker of writing." In linguistics Derrida draws crucially on Charles Sanders Peirce and Louis Hjelmslev. Husserl's phenomenology Derrida condemns as "the most radical and most critical restoration of the metaphysics of presence," but when he comes to the crucial effort to give coherence and viability to his conception of language he will resort to Husserl in an effort to patch over a nonnegotiable hiatus in his theory, an effort that fails, and in doing so reveals for what it is the tour de force that Derrida passes off as serious thought.[27]

Derrida speaks of "the absence of the signatory [subject], to say nothing of the absence of the referent," and says that "writing is the name of these two absences." The effort to find authority for the declaration of these two absences is the effort to achieve philosophical foundation for his thought. The first requirement of his effort is to deny the relevance of speech, sound, voice (and thus the organism) to the definition of language. Despite Saussure's inadequate conception of the sign, Derrida finds in his theory two arguments for excluding speech. The first of these is Saussure's statement that the linguistic signifier is not "phonic but incorporeal—constituted not by its material substance but the differences that separate its sound-image from all others." The second idea from Saussure is "the thesis of the *arbitrariness* of the sign." Derrida's reasoning here is that the phonic and the graphic signs are equally arbitrary and therefore one must exclude "any natural hierarchy among signifiers or orders of signifiers," i.e., the order of speech and the order of writing.[28] This argument in fact assumes that the relationship of the signifier to a signified, however it is defined, has no significance for the understanding of language: any acknowledgment of that relationship will give priority to the importance of speech.

While Derrida recognizes that to exclude sound, voice, organism, subject, is to exclude the object, the signified, he goes to Heidegger to further authorize this exclusion. It is with reason that Derrida can say, in *Positions*, "I sometimes have the feeling that the Heideggerean problematic is the most 'profound' and 'powerful' defense of what I attempt to put into question under the rubric of the *thought of presence.*" It may be argued that Derrida's thought is best defined by saying that he has accepted the thought of Heidegger while excluding the concept of being that all of Heidegger's thought labored to establish. When, in *Of Grammatology*, Derrida speaks of Heidegger's insistence on "the difference between being and the entity," we may reflect that while Heidegger's eventual failure to "think Being" might be taken to authorize our relinquishing "Being," it by no means authorizes our relinquishing "beings," or what Derrida calls the "entity" (the signified, or object), as Derrida, in effect, has done. Derrida says that in Heidegger "fundamentally nothing escapes the movement of the signifier and that, in the last instance, the difference between the signified and the signifier *is nothing.*"[29] This *"nothing"* certainly is not authorized by Heidegger; it is authorized by Heidegger only after Derrida has cleansed Heidegger's thought both of "Being" *and* of "beings," thereby transforming Heidegger's conception of language into pure solipsism.

Derrida turns eventually to Hjelmslev for authority to exclude the sound from language, and when he does so he is forced to confront the untenable foundation of his own thought. With reference to Hjelmslev's *Principles de grammaire générale*, Derrida says, "the very principle of [Hjelmslev's] glossematics as the formal science of language" is that "grammar is independent of semantics and phonology." What cannot be overemphasized is that when Derrida describes the subject matter of Hjelmslev's grammar we can say, with a crucial reservation, that Derrida presents his own conception of language: "The Copenhagen School thus frees a field of research: it becomes possible to direct attention not only to the purity of a form freed from all 'natural' bonds to a substance but also to everything that, in the stratification of language, depends on the substance of graphic expression." When Derrida eliminates both the subject and the signified, he necessarily falls back upon this abstract and ideal conception of language as pure form, which means that in Derrida's cosmos there is nothing but language. The problem for Derrida is that while he requires this conception of language as ideal and pure form, he wishes also to promote this exclusively linguistic conception to the status of philosophy. His ideal language must also be a language that has convincingly consumed the world. Only thus can "grammatology" replace philosophy. The difficulty with Hjelmslev's grammar, Derrida explains, is that it countenances other "regional" sciences, such as psychology, physiology, and sociology, as existing "parallel" with it, sciences which exist "rigorously outside linguistics."[30] Only if everything is subsumed under linguistics can "grammatology" become, or supplant, philosophy.

Derrida's problem is that he must bridge the ideal and the real without the help of deity. Language as ideal form must, somehow, after all, be brought into connection with "experience." The "experience" with which Derrida's abstract forms must be connected are simply speech and the "vulgar" concept of writing, but even this minimal requirement presents an insuperable problem. As Derrida says, "The concept of experience is most unwieldy here." The concept of experience, says Derrida, "belongs to the history of metaphysics and we can only use it under erasure [sous rature]." We will want to ask if he justifies the rature, for, as Derrida says, "it is the only way to escape 'empiricism' and the 'naive' critiques of experience at the same time." The possibility of putting experience "under erasure" must be made credible, and that will involve very strained contortions. We are told first that language as pure form is linked to experience through, of all things, "arche-writing": "However original and irreducible it might be, the 'form of expression' linked by correlation to the graphic 'substance of expression' remains very determined. It is very dependent and very derivative with regard to the arche-writing of which I speak. This arche-writing would be at work not only in the form and substance of graphic expression but also in those of non-graphic expression," that is, *speech.* Clearly this moves us back toward the organism, the subject, and logocentrism. That tendency is to be averted, presumably, by bringing Husserl back onto the scene, but more than a link with experience is involved. Derrida's invocation of Husserl is his essential effort to bestow philosophical status on "grammatology." It is now indicated for the first time that arche-writing involves "the parenthesizing of regions of experience or of the totality of natural experience." Parenthesizing, or bracketing, "the totality of natural experience," including the fact that one has a body—that is, assuming as a working hypothesis that these things do not exist—is the method of Husserl's reduction by which he sets the scene of phenomenological investigation, the observation of pure phenomena, or representations. The parenthesizing, says Derrida, "must discover a field of transcendental experience."[31] Now what Derrida discovers in this "field of transcendental experience" is nothing less than the totality of linguistic phenomena which he has posited, plus the concepts in which he describes them, plus, in other words, his entire theoretical construction. Put into relatively plain language, this would mean that carrying out Husserl's transcendental reduction would make possible the "discovery" of "arche-writing," "trace," and "differance." What are patently logical constructs now become *discoverable.*

Derrida does not say this directly. What he says is, "This [transcendental] experience is only accessible in so far as . . . one asks the question of the transcendental origin of the system itself, as a system of the objects of a science, and, correlatively, of the theoretical system which studies it." His direct reference here is to Hjelmslev's glossematics, but he makes clear in the same sentence that glossematics represents a general position that he shares, and the transcendental recourse is, of course, entirely his own. "It is," says Derrida, "to escape falling back into this naive objectivism [of the Copenhagen school] that I refer here to a transcendentality that I elsewhere put into question." As a matter of fact, Derrida's contrivance turns out to be an intellectual jackpot. The "undecidables," now become transcendentals, are safely beyond objective inquiry. But the rewards are far greater than that. By bracketing "all natural knowledge" and elevating the "undecidables" to transcendental status, "grammatology" becomes antecedent to all other knowledge. The sciences thus, not only partly, but completely, become derivative, and the description of the world as linguistic solipsism is justified.

Derrida's invocation of phenomenology is his supreme fiction. Unfortunately the fiction is indeed that, purely verbal. Everywhere else in his work Husserl and phenomenology are condemned. Nothing justifies the sudden flight to the Husserlian reduction except Derrida's desperate effort to have language both ways—isolated and related to some kind of reality—and to impose the usurpation of human knowledge by "grammatology." Furthermore, by invoking the transcendental, Derrida has with this linchpin of his theory restored the subject, which he everywhere denies.

The vacuity of the idea of the transcendental conception here may be suggested by recalling the significance of the reduction for Husserl. On the basis of what could be discovered within the transcendental realm, Husserl attempted to justify reestablishment of the external world and thus to establish the legitimacy of reason and of phenomenology as "rigorous science." The culminating effort to achieve this occurred in the fifth of Husserl's *Cartesian Meditations*. Derrida makes no effort at all to achieve this return to the world. Rather he remains within the linguistic solipsism that is always implicit in his work. Having pretended to ascend to the transcendental, he pretends to leave it simply by bracketing the bracketing of the reduction: the "experience" that is already bracketed and transcendental is written *sous rature* and the entire movement, though the philosophical status of grammatology depends on it, can be simply forgotten: "We must then *situate* as a simple moment of the discourse, the phenomenological reduction and the Husserlian reference to a transcendental experience."[32] This particular "moment" also requires attention. Derrida's implication is that illicit moments in his thought cannot invalidate what he is doing because he uses "logocentrism" but is not committed to it. He is exercising a process that uses logocentrism only to pass beyond it; because logocentrism is fundamentally fallacious, we cannot justly object to any fallacy in his arguments. In effect, there is no possibility of arguing with Derrida; he reasons, but his arguments are immune to the questioning of logic. The fact remains that what he pretends to be an uncommitted use of logocentrism proceeds from an assumption, and that assumption is totally without basis. If we are to admit of a process which uses logocentrism to pass beyond logocentrism, then there must be a comprehensible beyond. It must not be a void; we must not enter into oblivion. If it is not a void, then it must be in some way comprehensible. And if we are to attempt to pass beyond logocentrism to something other than a void, then there must be some evidence for such a comprehensible beyond. We have seen that evidence. It is the entirely fictional "arche-writing." Derrida's argument chases its tail, and it is an entirely mythic tail.

Deconstructionism labors in obedience to the need to reverse hierarchical oppositions, but to do so now in such a way that the reversal of oppositions will become an imperative and the single legitimation of intellectual pursuit. The purpose of reversals now is much more than to "unsettle the system." All philosophy, all thought, is to be brought to nothing in a single performance. So Derrida pretends earnestly now to take his reversals seriously and to validate them by a logical coherence and necessity that are not a requirement of his deconstructive method. From this flows all his philosophical labor, his quite humorless effort to establish theory.

The idea that there is no signified and that only language exists plays exactly the role of the mythic "arche-writing" in the reversal of "speech/writing." It is the means of "deconstructing" "signified/signifier," producing "signifier/~~signified~~ ('trace' which is 'nothing')." The difference this time is that the possibility of preserving the actual opposition in the reversal is precluded, and the reason is that we are here at the extreme outer limit of Derrida's system, the point at which admission of any "signified" would admit a circumambient world and permit it to encroach upon and contaminate a totally hermetic system. The system is exhaustively Hegelian, completely enclosed and self-sufficient. It is Hegel turned, not upside down, but inside out, a "concrete universal" from which the concrete has been evacuated.

The central purpose of this system, the real point of it all, is to achieve an implicit reversal of a truly fundamental hierarchical opposition. We can readily agree that, not all, but much of the thought of the past has assumed an opposition that we might write in this way: "IDENTITY/difference." Derrida's ultimate goal is "DIFFERENCE/~~identity~~." With that, the world deliquesces, collapses into traces, disappears. "PRESENCE/absence" becomes "ABSENCE/~~presence~~." "There are only everywhere, differences and traces of traces."[33]

Of Grammatology is Derrida's grammar, a foundation. But a foundation would be "presence," and so he writes a tour de force creating a non-grammar that is a denial of grammars and foundations. The logic of it is simply an inversion of the logic by which we may conceive the universe as an endless plenitude. It is all cleverness, intellectual legerdemain, and with none of the lightheartedness of Derrida's vaunted "free-play." It has relevance only as a curiosity. Its irrelevance to the study of literature becomes apparent when we consider what happens when quite respectable literary minds become mesmerized by the perverse energy of Derrida.

Paul de Man

For so long as we expect logical coherence in Paul de Man's *Allegories of Reading,* it is extremely difficult to read.[34] The difficulty disappears as soon as we understand that in every crucial articulation evidence is lacking or logic fails. Understanding that, we may watch in fascination a process in which ponderous scholarship is gathered in a collage that substitutes for reason. An analysis that makes this clear is necessary only because we cannot afford to temporize about this book. Either de Man's theory is of epochal moment or it is an unnecessary source of confusion within the contemporary welter of conflicting critical theories. The important parts of the text that I will examine here are representative.

Defects appear in the foundations of de Man's enterprise. Having identified "the rhetorical, figural potentiality of language with literature itself," de Man states his most general thesis: "a literary text simultaneously asserts and denies the authority of its own rhetorical mode." It is in this simultaneous assertion and denial that the text "deconstructs" itself. But the coexistence of the assertion and denial has a surprising effect. In connection with an example from Proust, which will be examined below, de Man says, "For if we then ask the obvious and simple next question, whether the rhetorical mode of the text in question is that of metaphor or metonymy, it is impossible to give an answer." The result is as follows: "Any question about the rhetorical mode of a literary text is always a rhetorical question which does not even know whether it is really questioning."[35] This statement is an abyss squirming with questions, and I will not attempt to confront all of them. The statement makes one problem inanely obvious. As de Man's argument will be concerned with a text's "own rhetorical mode," it is most disconcerting to be told that it is impossible to ask a definite and coherent question attempting to identify the rhetorical mode of a text. We may also want to know in what sense a question may question its questioning. To this question, the answer, perfectly clear and logical, is that there is no questioner to bear this uncertainty. Persons do nothing whatsoever; whatever is done is necessarily done by language itself. If we are here in the presence of Derrida, as we so often are in de Man, the absolute linguistic solipsism can lead us to the conclusion that what we assume to be persons in our environment are actually not persons but language. What de Man actually articulates in this connection is the more conservative "postmodernist" conception concerning fictional persons: "But even if we free ourselves of all false questions of intent and rightfully reduce the narrator to the status of a mere grammatical pronoun without which the narrative could not come into being, this subject remains endowed with a function that is not grammatical but rhetorical, in that it gives voice, so to speak, to a grammatical syntagm." De Man moves quickly to a further conclusion: "The narrator [of the passage from Proust] who tells us about the impossibility of metaphor is himself, or itself, a metaphor, the metaphor of a grammatical syntagm." [36]

Thus far two observations are appropriate. I think we might rather easily accept the function of the narrator as being rhetorical. We may at least hesitate over the statement that the narrator is a metaphor. We will come to see, however, that the purpose of this statement, which is not at all essential to de Man's argument, is to loosen up the reader's imagination in preparation for a further extension of the concept of metaphor for which de Man can provide no justification. Concerning another point, there must be no misunderstanding. If, as Derrida assumes, there is nothing in the world but language, de Man might seem justified in treating everything in the world as either grammar or rhetoric. The truth is that in de Man's conception of grammar referentiality is always implicit and his conception of rhetoric is, in one of its dimensions, traditional and narrow in a way that will not permit him to operate under the canopy of Derrida's linguistic solipsism. This is evident in the fact that de Man resorts to elaborate arguments of his own in the attempt to justify his terminology. The first chapter of the book is dedicated to an effort to legitimate an entirely new meaning of the word "rhetoric" which will permit de Man to apply the word "metaphor" to extralinguistic phenomena, to apply it, not to words, but to the things which words are about. His entire project will depend upon the effort to justify this profound confusion of categories.

De Man refers to two theoretical enterprises which he feels are favorable to his own but which he admits do not justify it. He refers to such work as that of Todorov in which grammatical categories are used to classify all textual elements larger than the sentence. De Man says, "The existence of grammatical structures, within and beyond the unit of the sentence, in literary texts is undeniable, and their description and classification are indispensable." He then acknowledges that "the question remains if and how figures of rhetoric can be included in such a taxonomy."[37] This seems prudent and modest enough, but what he does not acknowledge is that this taxonomy concerns strictly textual phenomena and that inclusion of rhetoric within it would by no means involve the extension of rhetorical categories beyond the text.

De Man turns next to speech-act theory, which seems at first more promising for his purposes. At issue here are two terms introduced by J. L. Austin, "illocutionary acts" and "perlocutionary acts." According to Austin, a perlocutionary act is a nonlinguistic act that may result from an illocutionary act, which is linguistic. It is not unreasonable to argue, as de Man does, that if "rhetoric" is a word for the entire area of persuasion, then speech-act theory may give rise to a new rhetoric, but it must be insisted that such a rhetoric would be descriptive of persuasive illocutionary acts, which are linguistic. The illocutionary realm described by such a grammar may "concern" the perlocutionary (the nonlinguistic), but if it describes that nonlinguistic realm, it will do so only as a means of formulating the rules for the use of illocutionary acts. In the suggestion, however, that such a rhetoric would describe the perlocutionary as a realm separable from language, de Man assumes what his entire introductory chapter is intended to prove. He acknowledges, furthermore, that speech-act theory can give rise to a new rhetoric only if rhetoric is taken as concerned with the entire area of persuasion and that this is irrelevant to his purposes in which "rhetoric" will be interpreted traditionally to designate "the study of tropes and figures."[38]

De Man's real question is the relationship between language and the nonlinguistic world, but he contrives for this to become what is in effect a red herring, the question of the possibility of identifying grammar with rhetoric. He points out that both tradition and American writers such as Kenneth Burke and Charles Sanders Peirce insist upon a distinction between grammar and rhetoric, and he acknowledges that they are probably right. Then de Man disorganizes the reader's powers of discrimination by the following sentence: "Only if the sign engendered meaning in the same way that the object engenders the sign, that is, *by representation*, would there be no need to distinguish between grammar and rhetoric."[39] Some of the problems here cannot be solved, but apparently "the object engenders the sign." So the object exists, which implies referentiality, which is also implicit in the concept of "representation." The idea of "representation" also restores the subject, as Heidegger made clear. In addition, de Man has missed Derrida's unquestionably valid point that if there is no subject there can be no object. The idea that the object engenders the sign *by representation* is inchoate. Over and again, de Man thus leads the reader into a realm of mystification in which, if we do not revolt, anything will come to seem possible. What the mystification conceals is that de Man's arguments do not rest upon a coherent theory of language but turn between diverse conceptions of language to suit erratic polemic purposes. This will become clearer as we proceed.

De Man eventually admits that he cannot establish a theoretical justification for arguing an interrelationship between grammar and rhetoric and, within the line of argument he has taken, this means that he cannot justify applying rhetorical terminology to extralinguistic phenomena. The question is, he says, "a difficulty which puts its concise theoretical exposition beyond my powers." Then he says, "I must retreat therefore into a pragmatic discourse and try to illustrate the tension between grammar and rhetoric in a few specific textual examples."[40] The suggestion is that he will be able to illustrate something for which he can find no theoretical explanation. We will want to watch this carefully.

Deconstruction will result from the "tension between grammar and rhetoric." By "grammar" de Man means literal language logically ordered. By "rhetoric," as has been pointed out, he means "figural language." Now the idea of literalness cannot be separated from the idea of referentiality, and without the idea of literalness there is no possible way of distinguishing between literal and figural language. There can be no doubt that for de Man literal language is in contact with the extralinguistic world. De Man's argument that literary language is not referential is only the argument that literary language is figurative language. A part of his preconceptual bias is indicated by the fact that he frequently speaks of "grammar" as "proper language." His introductory exposition deals with two literary texts. The first focuses on the last line of Yeats's "Among School Children": "How can we know the dancer from the dance?" This line, as de Man points out, is usually read figuratively. (We cannot possibly know the difference between the dancer and the dance.) He maintains, in a highly dubious and rather ludicrous reading of the poem, that the line can also be read literally. (We must be able to know the difference. Please tell us how.) We can see then, says de Man, that "two entirely incompatible readings can be made to hinge on one line, whose grammatical structure is devoid of ambiguity, but whose rhetorical mode turns the mood as well as the mode of the entire poem upside down." What has thus occurred, he explains, is "a rhetorization of grammar." This can have no real significance unless it is an observation of what is truly inherent in the poem and this necessity requires that de Man embrace another argument: "Nor can we in any way make a valid decision as to which of the readings can be given priority over the other." But it is not only that we cannot choose between them. We can be sure that both are inherent in the poem, and, much more than that, each is dependent on the other: "none can exist in the other's absence." One might protest that the literal reading did not exist at all until de Man contrived it. But for de Man the literal reading has always been there, secretly at work, whether we knew it or not, a part of the truth of things. If that were not true, then what he calls deconstruction would be not a discovery but an invention. But not at all: "The authority of the meaning engendered by the grammatical structure [the literal reading] is fully obscured by the duplicity of a figure." Invariably for de Man figurative language is somehow mendacious. The figure is deceitful; poems do lie, after all. But the "duplicity" of this figure is self-revealing. The figure "cries out for the differentiation that it conceals."[41] However questionable this may be, the essential point for the moment is that this analysis does not confront the basic problem inherent in de Man's theory.

It is only in de Man's second exemplary deconstruction that we confront the question of the application of rhetorical categories to extralinguistic phenomena. We will remember that this is to be justified, not theoretically, but pragmatically. The "pragmatic" exercise has been prepared for, obliquely, from the beginning of the introductory chapter. "There ought to be," says de Man, "another perspective, complementary to the first, in which metaphor, for example, would not be defined as a substitution but as a particular type of combination." It will eventually become clear that the new perspective would be "complementary to the first" because it would concern things rather than words. De Man goes on to say, "Research inspired by linguistics or, more narrowly, by syntactical studies, has begun to reveal this possibility—but it remains to be explored."[42] He then suggests that he will explore this possibility, and we have seen him acknowledge that his search for a theoretical justification fails. What he does not say at this point is that from the first paragraph of the book he has begun a process in which he will smuggle into the discussion a new definition of metaphor as "a particular type of combination."

For reasons that are not immediately obvious, the first three paragraphs of the book deal with debates, the result of which is that preference alternates between intrinsic and extrinsic criticism; this discussion concludes with the following statement: "The recurrent debate opposing intrinsic to extrinsic stands under the aegis of an inside/outside metaphor that is never being seriously questioned." This is the initial step in what will be for de Man a necessary strategy. For the moment, let us consider its immediate interest. It says that reference to the intrinsic/extrinsic opposition occurs "under the aegis" of an inside/outside metaphor, and the suggestion is very clear that if we "seriously questioned" the inside/outside metaphor we would find that there is something wrong with the intrinsic/extrinsic opposition, that is to say, that it is not an opposition. However, if we grant assumptions required by de Man's major thesis and by most of his analyses— the assumptions that objects exist separately from language and that language becomes literal by referring more or less directly to them— then there is nothing at all wrong with either of the two oppositions. These oppositions become questionable only with the assumption of the autonomy of language. But the autonomy of language precludes the possibility of literal language, and de Man must have it both ways. While committed to the idea of literalness, he wants later to discredit metaphor by attributing to it the error which Derrida attributes to the inside/outside opposition. Ignoring this quite insuperable problem, de Man assuages our discomfort by solving an easier one that is not essential to his argument. This incidental problem is that discrediting the inside/outside opposition also discredits the intrinsic/extrinsic opposition. His solution is to replace the terms "intrinsic" and "extrinsic" with the terms "semiology" and "semantics." His assumption is that the new terms will place the opposition beyond the reach of Derrida's deconstructive method. These terms, he explains, are "less likely to enter into the easy play of chiasmic reversals."[43] By this purely verbal means de Man can seem to protect his "intrinsic/extrinsic" opposition, while at the same time dramatizing the notion of the fallacy of the "inside/outside" opposition. The notion of this fallacy is important to him because he will shortly execute an arbitrary extension of the concept of metaphor in which metaphor becomes, he says, an "inside/outside" relationship, and this "inside/outside" relationship, because it is presumed to be somehow invalid, will be seen as the deconstructive power of what he calls "metaphor." Thus de Man's "deconstruction" will by implication have the authorization of Derrida. As a matter of fact, Derrida does not see the "inside/outside" dichotomy as a repressive hierarchy and he does not submit it to a reversal, "chiasmic" or otherwise. He simply sees the "inside/outside" relationship as inherent in the inevitable spatiality of language, and he maintains: "No philosophical language will ever be able to reduce the naturality of a spatial praxis in language." For Derrida the "inside/outside" dichotomy is seen as defective when it controls such relations as those to the "other" as person, or "the relation of Instants to each other," or "the relationship to Death." Certainly Derrida does not indict the "inside/outside" dichotomy as applied to actual spatial relations, and, obvious as this may be, the point has relevance to de Man's argument. De Man's purpose in introducing the theme of intrinsic and extrinsic criticism was to suggest, at some distance from his main argument, the presumed dangers of the "inside/outside" dichotomy, which will be mustered into surprising service in the next chapter, as we will now see.

Having "deconstructed" "Among School Children" in the dubious way which has been examined, de Man attempts to amplify the deconstruction. He says first that the poem is "about images or metaphors, and about the possibility of convergence between experiences of consciousness such as memory or emotions—what the poem calls passion, piety, and affection—and entities *accessible to the senses* [my italics] such as bodies, persons, or icons."[44] That seems unexceptionable, but de Man next says: "We return to the inside/outside model from which we started out. . . ." I want to note first that this is a typical example of the kind of thing that in de Man is so often a diversion. When we "return" to that "from which we started out," the wording seems to suggest some kind of inevitability or some kind of organic necessity in our return. Metaphors come to seem mysterious and strangely powerful. We do not just observe another occurrence of an earlier instance. We should also note that what we started out from was an inside/outside *metaphor;* in our "return" each of the two instances is called a *model.* As we proceed, the assumption that the two are the same will be used to support a fallacious logic. The difference between the two instances must be insisted on. If we may grant that in some sense the intrinsic/extrinsic dichotomy harbors an inside/ outside metaphor, it must be insisted that the inside/outside relationship which de Man sees as informing Yeats's poem is quite literal. Surely "memory and emotions" do really occur "inside" of us and "bodies, persons, or icons" that we observe or respond to do really occur externally, unmistakably "outside." In de Man's words, they are "accessible to the senses." According to de Man's description, the inside/outside relationship is unquestionably real; to describe it as an inside/outside relationship is to speak literally about phenomena external to language. To speak of this literal description of a spatial relationship as a "model" has the single purpose of easing a transformation by which the literal will become a metaphor, licensing de Man to speak of "rhetoric" where none exists. But before that remarkable change occurs, we confront other problems. The complete sentence with which we are concerned is as follows: "We return to the inside/ outside model from which we started out and which the poem puts into question by means of a syntactical device (the question) made to operate on a grammatical as well as on a rhetorical level." The argument that the question operates on a grammatical level is at least dubious, as I have indicated heretofore, but let us assume that it is valid. What we want first to know is in what sense the inside/outside relationship is put into question. It is, in fact, the purpose of the final stanza to do that questioning. The inside/outside relationship is registered in the lines which I have italicized below. The unitalicized lines put the relationship into question:

> Labor is blossoming or dancing where
> *The body is not bruised to pleasure soul,*
> *Nor beauty born out of its own despair,*
> *Nor blear-eyed wisdom out of midnight oil.*
> O chestnut tree, great-rooted blossomer,
> Are you the leaf, the blossom, or the bole?
> *O body swayed to music, O brightening glance,*
> How can we know the dancer from the dance?

The questioning of the inside/outside relationship occurs in both of the readings that de Man accepts. The generally accepted figurative reading denies that we can know the difference between the dancer and the dance. De Man's literal reading acknowledges that at least temporarily we do not know the difference. The questioning does not otherwise occur. Yet, for de Man the "deconstruction" is not Yeats's but his own. This is achieved abruptly. The inside/outside relationship which he has previously described as literal, thoroughly in accord with his own embrace of literalness and "proper" language, now becomes necessarily subject to the ambiguity that the autonomy of language bestows on all language and thus in its essentially rhetorical, nonliteral nature may be infected by the uncertainty lodged in adjacent locutions, specifically that conflict of grammar and rhetoric that he feels he has found in the final line of the poem: "The couple grammar/rhetoric, certainly not a binary opposition since they in no way exclude each other, disrupts and confuses the neat antithesis of the inside/outside pattern." De Man is now ready to execute the sleight of hand by which "the illocutionary speech act becomes a perlocutionary actual act." For de Man, in other words, the linguistic act will become, arbitrarily and incoherently, a nonlinguistic act, a move that confounds entirely the basic conception of speech-act theory, permitting the transportation of "rhetoric" into any realm in which one may wish to find it. His argument is as follows: "We can transfer this scheme [the inside/outside relationship] to the act of reading and interpretation." The justification for this is a jugglery of words: "By reading we get, as we say, *inside* a text that was first something alien to us and which we now make our own by an act of understanding. But this understanding becomes at once the representation of an extratextual meaning."[45] As the result of this "transfer," and within four lines, the act of reading becomes "the metaphor of reading." Now reading is often a reading *of* metaphor, and we may read in one way or in many others, just as we may eat one food or many others, and these diverse possibilities in no way elevate either "eating" or "reading" into metaphorical status or deprive these activities of actuality. It is by the transfer of a literal inside/outside relationship called a "model" to another literal inside/outside relationship that de Man pretends to have established the act of reading as a metaphor. De Man's second exemplary "deconstruction" is totally dependent upon this totally spurious transformation.

His second analysis concerns a passage from *À la recherche du temps perdu* in which the young Marcel, after resisting his aunt's insistence that he go out of doors, argues that he can know the out of doors best by reading a book within doors. De Man tells us that this passage which praises reading is a passage praising metaphor and therefore preferring metaphor over metonymy. He next demonstrates that this passage, presumably in praise of metaphor, actually employs chiefly metonymy. De Man then piously concludes, "After the rhetorical reading of the Proust passage, we can no longer believe the assertion made in this passage about the intrinsic, metaphysical superiority of metaphor over metonymy." [46]

What we eventually discover is that de Man is persistently hostile to figurative language and, by the implication of his own terminology, to literature. He quotes the following sentence from Proust: "The dark cool of my room was to the full sunlight of the street what the shadow is to the sunray, that is to say equally luminous." With severity, de Man says, "In a logic dominated by truth and error the equation is absurd, since it is the difference of luminosity that distinguishes between shadow and light; 'that is to say' ('c'est à dire') in the quotation is precisely what cannot be said." In the pedantry of this there is a faint suggestion of the bourgeois gentleman discovering that he speaks prose. De Man, now passionate advocate of strict logic, is shaken by what he has discovered: "One should ask how a blindness comes into being that allows for a statement in which truth and falsehood are completely subverted to be accepted as true without resistance." [47]

One of the works which de Man "deconstructs" at great length is Nietzsche's *The Birth of Tragedy*. According to de Man the work both argues for and embodies, or attempts to embody, what de Man calls a "genetic" principle. This conception, presumably because it is irredeemably fallacious, is a deconstructive factor within the work and, in the course of Nietzsche's argument, creates a "semantic dissonance" that "compels the reader to enter into an apparently endless process of deconstruction." It is this conception of the genetic that we should first examine. De Man, in effect, recognizes that the conception is virtually omnipresent. It "underlies all historical narrative." He says that even Michel Foucault and Jacques Derrida, in their "attempts to see the conceptual crisis of language that figures so prominently in contemporary philosophy, as closing of a historical period," fall within the pattern of texts "which by their own structure and their own statement, lay the foundation for the genetic conception of history." [48] Apparently the conception is essential to all explanatory discourse. We must see the theoretical basis of de Man's own deconstructive project as embodying this principle: a "tension" between "rhetoric and grammar" gives rise to "endless deconstructions."

A major concern of de Man's is the connection between the genetic principle and Romanticism: "Romanticism itself is generally understood as the passage from a mimetic to a genetic concept of art and literature." The Romantic vision is one in which "'all things below' are said to be part of a chain of being underway to its teleological end." De Man does not reject this; he acknowledges "the emergence of the genetic pattern within the Romantic imagination and Romantic rhetoric." On the other hand, de Man suspects that "the so-called Romantics came closer than we do to undermining the absolute authority of this system," i.e., the "logocentric" system of which the genetic concept, says de Man, is a part. Now de Man sees in this very possibility evidence of awesomely powerful implications in the presence, or absence, of the genetic concept, and this involves him in a startling bit of reasoning. De Man says, "The ultimate test or 'proof' of the fact that Romanticism puts the genetic pattern of history in question would then be the impossibility of writing a history of Romanticism."[49] Our very astonishment calls for restatement of this egregious logic: We cannot write a history of a period in which the major writers, "the so-called Romantics," reject the genetic principle, and therefore, reject history. As de Man observes that "no truly dialectical history of Romanticism has been written," we are to conclude, presumably, that the question is settled. The topic is a digression, or a diversion, but it is representative of the reasoning in the work.

The earliest draft of *The Birth of Tragedy* consisted of only the first fifteen sections.[50] Here Nietzsche described Attic tragedy as the conjunction and harmony of the Apollonian and Dionysian principles. Apollo, god of sculpture, is "the god of all plastic energies," "the glorious divine image of the *principium individuationis.*"[51] Dionysos contrasts as the god of the nonimagistic art of music.[52] Apollo and Dionysos correspond, respectively, to "the separate art worlds of *dreams and intoxication.*" Attic tragedy, reaching its highest development in Sophocles, is "an equally Dionysian and Apollonian form of art." The decline and eventual disappearance of Attic tragedy is far advanced in the work of Euripides under the influence of "a new Orpheus," who is Socrates, "the mystagogue of science," who is "the type of the *theoretical man.*"[53] In the first fifteen sections Nietzsche's writing is unexceptionable, close to the excellence of his best performance. Unfortunately he decided to write an additional ten sections arguing the inevitability of the rebirth of tragedy. Here his incontinent enthusiasm for his earliest heroes, Schopenhauer and Wagner, gives rise to obvious excesses. Sections 16 through 25 have made the work vulnerable to criticisms, none of which has been more intolerant than Nietzsche's own. Nietzsche says of the book, "I consider it badly written, ponderous, embarrassing, image-mad and image-confused, sentimental, in places saccharine to the point of effeminacy, uneven in tempo, without the will of logical cleanliness, very convinced and therefore disdainful of proof, mistrustful even of the *propriety* of proof. . . ." After further abuse of the book, Nietzsche takes some pride in the fact that it was persuasive and that it gave the first expression to "an instinct that aligned itself with life and that discovered for itself a fundamentally opposite doctrine and valuation of life." Of the doctrine aligning itself with life Nietzsche says, "I called it Dionysian." [54] It may be asked if de Man, who does not mention Nietzsche's criticism, has more convincingly described the defects of the book or explained them better.

The first requirement of de Man's argument is that he establish *The Birth of Tragedy* as sustaining the genetic concept. This he finds in the relationship between Dionysos and Apollo: "The starting point Dionysos contains within itself the end-point, the Apollonian work of art, and governs the dialectical pathway that leads from one to the other." [55] The fact is that most of Nietzsche's references to the two deities, or principles, exclude the genetic relationship. There exists between them "a tremendous opposition, in origin and aims." [56] The two principles "continually incite each other to new and more powerful births." Nietzsche says that his argument is "in contrast to all those who are intent on deriving the arts from one exclusive principle." The powers of dreams, which are identified with Apollo, are "omnipotent art impulses." He speaks of "the strife of these two hostile principles." In tragedy they combine in "a sweeping opposition of styles." In the Doric the Apollonian is "a permanent military encampment" against the incursions of the Dionysian. The Apollonian's opposition to the Dionysian is violent: it "tears us out of the Dionysian universality" and "tears man from his orgiastic self-annihilation." The two principles "perpetuate an antagonism only superficially reconciled by the common term 'art'." So opposed are the two principles that their eventual combination in Attic tragedy seems unlikely: "all truly aesthetic spectators will confirm that among the peculiar effects of tragedy this coexistence is the most remarkable." While the two principles are more frequently opposed, seen, indeed, as antithetical, a few passages may be taken as embodying the genetic relationship.

As various writers have pointed out, Dionysos has priority. Nietzsche speaks of "the Dionysian basic ground of the world." Furthermore, Apollonian manifestations are "appearances in which Dionysos objectifies himself." Unless Dionysos is not the origin of that in which he objectifies himself, then unmistakably the relationship is conceived at this point as genetic. In any event, there is little reason for doubt that conceptual contradictions reflected here are not reconciled. Surely Nietzsche's choice of the gods to represent the principles with which he is concerned is designed to relieve him of the necessity of the kind of ultimate systematization that de Man reads into the book. While de Man does not mention the actual oppositions between the Dionysian and Apollonian, he does acknowledge that the "parental imagery of *The Birth of Tragedy* is inconsistent."[57] The point to be insisted on is that, if de Man's "deconstruction" has any merit at all, the genetic conception must have a very firm grip upon Nietzsche's imagination and must be somehow a governing principle of the entire work. The text does not suggest this.

If de Man virtually ignores the conceptual contradictions that I have emphasized, he also advances an argument that may be taken to justify his discounting the importance of logical conflicts generally. It is important to keep in mind that if de Man's analysis is to depend upon the observation of logical defects, then "deconstruction" is nothing new. The fact remains, however, that de Man is always ultimately concerned with logical conflicts; his point is that "rhetoric" is in logical conflict with "grammar." Nevertheless, de Man provides a formulation which is intended to establish that deconstruction is something new and that truth will out on the basis of something other than the observation of logical defects. This formulation occurs in the course of an argument in which, surprisingly, de Man discounts the importance of the single obvious genetic relationship treated by Nietzsche, the historical genesis in which tragedy is destroyed by the Socratic spirit and restored in the music of Wagner. Nietzsche's treatment of this genetic development de Man discusses in two perspectives, with countervalent results. On one hand he disparages the passage in which Nietzsche treats the Wagnerian restoral as "the reverse process" of the decline of the Dionysian spirit.[58] Passages of this kind, says de Man, "are valueless as arguments" since they assume that "the actual events of history are founded in formal symmetries." As the result, he says, though he does not demonstrate the point, "the narrative links are so weak that one may feel tempted to put the unity of the text in question for purely philological reasons," i.e., reasons involving logical inadequacies of one sort or another. De Man points out that, on the other hand, the historical genesis is not merely a matter of "formal symmetries," but involves a logic of a sort and has a content. There is a movement from Socrates to Wagner (Dionysos) which is a movement from science to art, or "from the most extreme of epistemological constraint to the liberating influence of German music." Now this movement and this logic involve an "ambivalence of the epistemological moment," an "epistemological paradox." The paradox consists in the following: "It can be shown," says de Man, "that whenever an art form is being discussed, the three modes represented by Dionysos, Apollo, and Socrates are always simultaneously present and that it is impossible to mention one of them without at least implying the others." However, this is not "shown," either by de Man or by Nietzsche. De Man goes on to support this by saying: "The Dionysian moments always occur in revolt against the tyranny or as a result of the failure of the Socratic claim to knowledge." De Man's wording here would require us to reason that wherever the Dionysian occurs, the Socratic has simply failed, being part of a system that was in place from the beginning. This systematizes Nietzsche. Beyond associating the Socratic with the scientific, he says nothing about its origin and certainly does not find its origin in either the Dionysian or the Apollonian, and it could not have preceded them. However, let us suppose that the three principles, as de Man maintains, are always present when one of them is present and that the conjunction of the Dionysian and Socratic principles constitutes an "epistemological paradox." We might assume that this paradox would pose deconstructive possibilities. Not at all, says de Man: "Nietzsche is entirely in control of this problem and can state it with full thematic clarity, precisely in describing the transformation of the Socratic into the Wagnerian man." Furthermore, "the genetic structure of *The Birth of Tragedy* is not affected, literally or rhetorically, by the epistemological paradox that it contains."[59]

The presumed rejection of conceptual contradiction as the basis for "deconstruction" culminates in a formulation that is fundamental to de Man's project. He says, "We must look further in order to discover whether the genetic pattern of *The Birth of Tragedy* is substantial (i.e., motivated by thematic statement considered as *meaning*) or rhetorical (i.e., motivated by thematic statement considered as *structure*)."[60] What de Man is maintaining here is that "thematic statement considered as meaning" is not the deconstructing element. What deconstructs is rhetoric, not logic. So indirectly, by implication, de Man is executing a move that is very curious but that is necessary to his theory. Just as the act of reading becomes "metaphor," the concept of the genetic must now become "rhetoric," "thematic statement considered as structure." Obviously this argument, and, especially if it were made explicit, would be extremely hard to maintain. A bit later de Man will pose as illustrating his argument in a passage from Nietzsche which is in fact rhetorical and exaggerated, but this passage does not maintain the genetic concept; it maintains that music is unbearable unless mediated by words and images.

The purpose of de Man's formulation here is to adapt the grammar-rhetoric conflict to the analysis of *The Birth of Tragedy*. Those thematic parts of the work we consider to have "substance," and "meaning" correspond to "grammar" or "proper language." The thematic parts of the work that we find to be deficient of meaning we may consider to be "structure," and such "structure," even though it may not be constituted by figural language, we may call "rhetoric." De Man's task will be to show that the passages considered deficient in meaning somehow subvert the passages that otherwise might be considered to have "substance" or "meaning." Such a mechanism is nowhere demonstrated. Of course, we may acknowledge that weak passages in a work tend to discredit the work as a whole and in that respect have the effect of discrediting the strong passages. But if that is all there is to the argument, "deconstruction" is nothing new and it does not go beyond Nietzsche's criticism of the work.

Throughout his analysis de Man deals with thematic statement considered as meaning, with conceptual and logical inadequacies. His discussion is turgid, almost impenetrable; I will attempt to disentangle the crucial arguments, though these are hardly more than suggestions the implications of which are never decisively articulated. Much of de Man's concern focuses on the Dionysos-Apollo relationship. It is true that possibilities of confusion stem from the introduction in section 16 of a long passage from Schopenhauer maintaining that music is "an immediate copy of the will itself." As de Man points out, the idea of "an unmediated representation" is "a logical absurdity." On one hand he quotes an opinion that in Nietzsche this idea is "never accepted without reservations, but also never truly contested." On the other hand, de Man unmistakably implies that Nietzsche affirms the idea: "Schopenhauer's definition of music as being the 'unmediated image of the will' . . . rests in the power and authority of the will as subject. Nietzsche can therefore only write from the point of view, as it were, of the will." This has been prepared for by the following statement: "What Nietzsche calls, following Schopenhauer, the 'Will' is still a subject, a consciousness capable of knowing what it can and what it cannot tolerate, capable of knowing its own volition." Nowhere in the book does Nietzsche credit the significance of the idea of a personal will in art. What he does say about the personal will is as follows: "We know the subjective artist only as the poor artist, and throughout the entire range of art we demand first of all the conquest of the subjective, redemption from the 'ego', and the silencing of the individual will and desire." Elsewhere he says, "The willing individual that furthers his own egotistic ends, can be conceived of only as the antagonist, not as the origin of art. Insofar as the subject is the artist, however, he has already been released from his individual will."[61]

De Man's mistaken insistence upon Nietzsche's commitment to the personal will permits him to speak of "the Dionysian subject," which in the context of *The Birth of Tragedy* is essentially a self-contradictory concept, as the tendency of the Dionysian is to release one from his individuality. The phrase occurs in a passage that can serve as an illustration of the fact that we confront far greater problems in the text of de Man than we do in that of Nietzsche:

> The categories of truth and falsehood can only be introduced by the Dionysian subject which, from that moment on, stands itself under the aegis of this polarity. Empowered, but also compelled to decide on matters of truth and falsehood—as when it allows itself to refer to the Apollonian as a lie ("suffering is somehow being lied away out of the traits of nature . . .")—it has to run the risk of having to decree the loss of its own claim to truth.[62]

In the locution "as when it allows itself to refer . . ." the referring that is mentioned is done by Nietzsche, who thus becomes the "Dionysian subject," which seems hardly fair and is misleading. Strictly speaking the Dionysian principle can know only truth; falsehood is possible only for the Apollonian articulations of image and language. The rest of the passage is loaded with implications of the duplicity of the Dionysian and this is achieved by a reasoning which, even if we grant its erroneous assumptions, is inane: since the Dionysian has created the categories of truth and falsehood, it has created the possibility that it (Nietzsche) may have to acknowledge its own falsehood, assuming it is indeed false. This hardly justifies de Man's ominous suggestion.

De Man's reading that convicts the Dionysian of falsehood is clearly contrived. This occurs in connection with a passage in which Nietzsche discusses "three stages of illusion" by which the will, the "universal" will, seduces its creatures. The third of these illusions is "the metaphysical comfort that beneath the whirl of phenomena eternal life flows on indestructibly." Of this passage de Man says, "Contrary to all earlier claims, the Dionysian is then called one stage of delusion." This is patently an impossible reading. Of the three stages of illusion, Nietzsche says "All that we call culture is made up of these stimulants." Culture is the Apollonian realm. Elsewhere Nietzsche explains the "metaphysical consolation" in this way: "The metaphysical joy in the tragic is a translation of the instinctive unconscious Dionysian wisdom into the language of images," i.e., into the Apollonian. It is the Apollonian image, in myth, that brings to us the illusion and the comfort: "Apollo overcomes the suffering of the individual by the radiant glorification of the *eternity of the phenomenon:* here beauty triumphs over the suffering inherent in life." De Man also makes much of the conception of the Apollonian as "appearance," "illusion," and therefore "lie," implying "a discredited concept of representation." Nietzsche does refer repeatedly to the Apollonian as illusion, but he also explains the illusion in a way that preserves the authenticity of the Apollonian. He says that "the lie of culture," which is the Apollonian, is that it "poses as if it were the only reality." [63] The Apollonian, then, is a reality; it becomes illusion and lie only in its concealing the Dionysian.

It would seem clear that only by his own "misreading" and his own invention has de Man discredited "the category of representation that underlies the narrative mode and the category of the subject that supports the all-pervading hortatory voice" in *The Birth of Tragedy.* (We are aware, of course, that deconstructionism discredits the "category of the subject," regardless of what may or may not be found in Nietzsche's text.) It is true, however, that in "the preparatory outlines of *The Birth of Tragedy*" de Man discovers a statement that may be taken as demolishing the Apollonian-Dionysian relationship insofar as it has the genetic character which de Man attributes to it. The pertinent passages are as follows: "We are not entitled to transfer purposeful systems of action . . . into the nature of things" and "In the realm of nature and of necessity, all teleological hypotheses are absurd."[64] It is perhaps significant that the passage de Man quotes is in the subjunctive and at this time in Nietzsche's career may be taken as speculative, but if what it says is actually affirmed, de Man's conclusion is justified: "The radical separation of origin from purpose . . . that is established here eliminates all possible claim at genetic totalization."[65] However, this only affirms the dominant way of characterizing the Dionysian-Apollonian relationship within the text, and, furthermore, we are here in the realm of traditional scholarship, far from the subtleties of "deconstruction." De Man's contention is that such external evidences only corroborate his "deconstruction" of the text, which has yet to be established.

De Man finds also in a lateral but external source another passage that he says is in conflict with the text. It is as follows: "One could object that I myself have declared that the 'Will' receives an increasingly adequate symbolic expression in music. To this I reply, in a sentence that summarizes a basic principle of aesthetics: *the will is the object of music, but not its origin.*" Of this De Man says: "This sentence could never have stood in the final version if *The Birth of Tragedy* had to survive as a text." This is a strange comment, for the external passage says precisely what is said in a passage which is from the text and which de Man has quoted a few lines earlier: "One should here distinguish as sharply as possible the notion of essence from that of appearance, for the very nature of music excludes that it be the will. This would eliminate it from the realm of art altogether, for the will is in essence the nonaesthetic. But music *appears* as will" [my italics], i.e., it represents the will.[66] Both statements affirm that music is not the will, but represents the will, and is an aesthetic representation of a nonaesthetic object. In this case de Man's citation of external material has no significance at all.

Abruptly at one point, and without obvious connection with what has gone before, de Man says, "Or what are we to make of the theory of dissonance that comes to the fore near the end of the text and functions there as a dynamic and temporal principle that can no longer be called genetic?" This theory of dissonance is introduced by Nietzsche in this way: "How can the ugly and the disharmonic, the content of the tragic myth, stimulate aesthetic pleasure?" The basis of de Man's reasoning that dissonance must be excluded from the genetic cannot be identified. If the dissonance is to be excluded from the genetic because it is a dynamic and temporal principle, then all music must be excluded for the same reason. De Man does not really mean that the "theory" functions as a "dynamic and temporal principle." That would be entirely unintelligible. If the dissonance is to be excluded from the genetic on the basis of the text, then presumably we would have to find that this dissonance is in some way at discord with, incompatible with, the genetic "source." What Nietzsche tells us of the source is that in the Dionysian festival the individual "succumbed to the self-oblivion of the Dionysian states." Then "*Excess* revealed itself as truth. Contradiction, the bliss born of pain, spoke out from the very heart of nature." Over and again Nietzsche asserts "the contradiction at the heart of the world." And the Dionysian artist "has identified himself with the primal unity, its pain and contradiction." Musical dissonance is entirely in accord with the character of what the text maintains to be its genetic source. Immediately after declaring that musical dissonance can no longer be called genetic, de Man says, quite obscurely, "The semantic dissonance of *The Birth of Tragedy* is precisely this residue of meaning [the theory of musical dissonance?] that remains beyond the reach of the text's own logic and compels the reader to enter into an apparently endless process of deconstruction."[67] It has been made clear, however, that none of the deconstructions in this "endless process" will bear close examination. To be sure, we have examined only arguments concerned with "thematic statement considered as meaning," with conceptual and logical incompatibilities.

De Man is interested in something else, which he treats very obscurely. Early on de Man tells us that the genetic principle must be seen as a "system, with all the conceptual categories that it implies (subject, intent, negation, totalization, supported by the underlying metaphysical categories of identity and presence)." What this means is that Nietzsche's thought in *The Birth of Tragedy* is what the "deconstructionists" call "logocentrism." That it is such should be obvious from the fact that his thought proceeds propositionally and, furthermore, deals in oppositions. So we may be puzzled by the cultivation of mystery, when, in preparation to expand on the logocentric dimensions of Nietzsche's thought, de Man tells us that "The main theoretical speculations on language and art that originated at the time of *The Birth of Tragedy* have not been included in the final version." De Man then cites a letter to Rhode transmitting the lecture "Socrates and Tragedy." He quotes Nietzsche as saying, "'a curious metaphysics of art, which serves as background [to the main text of *The Birth of Tragedy*], is more or less my property, that is to say *real* estate [*Grundbesitz*], though not yet circulating, monetary, and consumed property'."[68] De Man concludes that "real estate" is one of the "main theoretical speculations on language and art" that "have not been included in the final version," and he then turns to the "final version" to identify this speculation; he has no other source. He says, "Everything seems to suggest that this 'property' stems indeed from the dispossession of the word in favor of music."[69] There is no doubt that this dispossession occurs, and it is fundamental. Nietzsche says,

> Language can never adequately render the cosmic symbolism of music, because music stands in symbolic relation to the primordial contradiction and primordial pain in the heart of the primal unity, and therefore symbolizes a sphere which is beyond and prior to all phenomena. Rather, all phenomena, compared with it, are merely symbols: hence *language,* as the organ and symbol of phenomena, can never by any means disclose the innermost heart of music; language, in its attempt to imitate it, can only be in superficial contact with music; while all the eloquence of lyric poetry cannot bring the latter one step nearer to us.[70]

Music gives rise to the tragic myth, but it does so, not in words, but in images: "music at its highest stage must seek to attain also to its highest objectification in images." And "the myth does not at all obtain adequate objectification in the spoken word." The alienation of language from myth is radical. Nothing could be more fundamental to *The Birth of Tragedy.* Despite this, de Man elaborates the dispossession of language by music in the following terms: "The property rights over truth that belong, by philosophical authority [this is intended as irony], to the power of language as statement, are transferred to the power of *language as voice and melody*" [my italics]. Insofar as voice, in addition to melody, may constitute the music which dispossesses language in this context, voice can have nothing at all to do with language. De Man attempts here to confine Nietzsche within the margins of "logocentrism" as it is conceived by Derrida, for whom logocentrism is always a linguistic product. De Man goes on to suggest a comparison between the two dichotomies "music/language" and "voice/writing," the latter of which Derrida is assumed to have deconstructed. These dichotomies exist, however, in entirely different categories. De Man is, nevertheless, correct in seeing that Nietzsche's conception of music convicts him of "ontology" and in this sense places him in the logocentric camp. This, however, is followed by a non sequitur: "It also recovers the possibility of language to reach full and substantial meaning."[71] *The Birth of Tragedy* denies this possibility over and over again.

De Man's verbal duplicity is not necessary to identify the Nietzsche of *The Birth of Tragedy* as a logocentric writer. But apparently—and we cannot be entirely certain about this—de Man wishes to say something further about Nietzsche and logocentrism. De Man says, "A great deal of evidence points to the likelihood that Nietzsche might be in the grip of a powerful assumption about the nature of language, bound to control his conceptual and rhetorical discourse regardless of whether the author is aware of it or not." Surely de Man is not being mysterious again about the identification of Nietzsche's thought as logocentric. And, as we have seen, de Man maintains that Nietzsche's final thought on language does not appear in the "final version." De Man tells us that the deconstruction that occurs within the text results from a statement that is not to be found in the text but which may be derived from it. It is a "metalinguistic" statement "about the rhetorical nature of language." De Man goes on to say that this "nonauthoritative secondary statement that results from the reading will have to be a statement about the *limitations of textual authority*" [my italics].[72] Now an essential characteristic of a truly logocentric writer is that he does *not* recognize "the limitations of textual authority." So what de Man apparently wants to suggest is that while Nietzsche in *The Birth of Tragedy* is a logocentric writer and thinker, he has also, in this early work, conceived of "logocentrism," and to have this concept is in part to escape from logocentrism and at least to conceive of the limitations of textual authority. De Man does not say this and nowhere does he provide evidence of Nietzsche's conception of logocentrism in *The Birth of Tragedy*. Whatever the unexpressed "statement" is, it is, as de Man modestly says, "nonauthoritative and secondary." The point is that if de Man did intend to attribute the concept of logocentrism to Nietzsche, we would find it at least conceivable that the logocentric concept recognizing the limitations of textual authority might effectively conflict with a logocentric practice that does not acknowledge such limitations. We could at least understand what de Man means when he says that deconstruction occurs "between, on the one hand, metalinguistic statements about the rhetorical nature of language and, on the other hand, a rhetorical praxis that puts these statements into question."[73] What may be de Man's most coherent argument for a disruptive influence upon the text is never made explicit, perhaps because the evidence for it is lacking, or because he wants to use this argument in connection with the later Nietzsche, as we shall see, and would find it awkward to use it in both cases.

Throughout his discussion, de Man makes references to rhetorical aspects of *The Birth of Tragedy*. On one hand it is "considered to be one of Nietzsche's most unified texts," but on the other "the diachronic successive structure . . . is an illusion."[74] We are not told what accounts for this failure of successive structure, and to attempt such an explanation would involve de Man in patent contradiction. If Nietzsche has a fully developed genetic, i.e., logocentric, thesis, it should lend itself to diachronic succession and closure. But to the degree that the genetic thesis is qualified and limited, de Man's own thesis is imperiled. If Nietzsche has conceived of logocentrism as opposed to being a blind victim of logocentrism, he cannot be committed to the genetic principle, which de Man has identified with logocentrism. So in this connection we are not permitted to observe the mechanism by which thematic statement considered as structure deconstructs.

Persistently de Man treats Nietzsche's rhetoric as a culpable strategy of deceit. *The Birth of Tragedy* is "a harangue that combines the seductive power of a genetic narrative [achieved through rhetorical inducements] with the rhetorical complicity of a sermon."[75] The most notable instance of Nietzsche's rhetorical excess occurs in the course of his contention that the music of the third act of Wagner's *Tristan and Isolde* would result in unbearable power if myth, if word and image, did not intervene to protect the audience.[76] This passage, says de Man, "has all the trappings of the statement made in bad faith: parallel rhetorical questions, an abundance of clichés, obvious catering to its audience." How is this excess to be accounted for? We are now told that Nietzsche is simply attempting to conceal the fact that "the 'deadly' power of music is a myth that cannot withstand the ridicule of literal description." We are to believe that rhetoric is not only an instrument here; it is also a cause. De Man says, "Nietzsche is compelled by the rhetorical mode of his text to present it [the myth] in the absurdity of its facticity."[77] De Man gives us no inkling of explanation as to how "a rhetorical mode" can compel Nietzsche to present any thematic matter at all, much less a myth which, by implication, he knows to be false. One might like to suggest that the rhetorical excess here is to be explained by the facts, first, that Nietzsche actually was profoundly moved by the music and, second, that he was deeply impressed by Wagner, greatly valued the friendship of the older man, and so leapt at the opportunity to flatter him. Such an explanation is forbidden because it introduces the "subject," Nietzsche the human being, and deconstructionism has abolished the category of the subject. It follows that whatever is to be explained is to be explained by dynamisms of language.

Concerning the possibility that Nietzsche recognizes the facticity of the myth and is compelled to present it by the rhetorical mode of his discourse, it is relevant to point out that the myth in its excessively rhetorical presentation in Section 21 is simply an adaptation and interpretation of a "myth" he had presented in Section 9, explaining that the Apollonian element of tragedy is necessary to protect the reader from the extremes of Dionysian possibility. This first version of the myth must be as factitious as the second, but it gives rise, not to rhetorical excess, but to one of Nietzsche's most effective metaphors: "When after a forceful attempt to gaze on the sun we turn away blinded, we see dark-colored spots before our eyes, as a cure, as it were. Conversely, the bright image projections of the Sophoclean hero—in short, the Apollonian aspect of the mask—are necessary effects of a glance into the inside and terrors of nature; as it were, luminous spots to cure eyes damaged by gruesome night." [78]

During the course of de Man's discussion, his guiding thesis, that involving the tension between "rhetoric" and "grammar," has been waiting in the wings to make its appearance in the final paragraph. But along the way its appearance is prepared for, and by a device to which one must take the gravest exception. We are provided with yet another extension of the meaning of the word "metaphor," comparable to, but not the same as, the earlier extension of the term to apply to the act of reading. De Man, we recall, argues that the relationship between the Apollonian and the Dionysian is genetic; the Apollonian is the teleological goal of the Dionysian. But also he maintains that the Apollonian relates to the Dionysian as the Appearance relates to the Thing. The Apollonian, de Man argues, may be taken as representing the Dionysian and for de Man, therefore, the Apollonian is a metaphor for the Dionysian. Apollo is metaphor, Dionysos is meaning. "There is little difficulty," says de Man, "in matching the two mythological poles, Dionysos and Apollo, with the categories of appearance and its antithesis, or with the relationship between metaphorical and proper language." [79] It must be recognized that to speak of Apollo as a metaphor for Dionysos is a perversion of language. "Metaphor," which is a word for a certain kind of relationship between words and between words and things, is now applied to things which are presumably not words but the entities, fictional or real, which words represent. The deconstructionist contention that all things are language, even if it is in a sense true, cannot possibly be taken to legitimate the confusion of categories which occurs here. De Man has abandoned "proper language" for "rhetorical language." He uses the word "metaphor" metaphorically, and when he does so the word loses all its specificity, becomes meaningless. By de Man's reasoning, the son becomes a metaphor for the father, the bread for the dough, the product for the labor, the chicken for the egg. We can do anything with words, of course, but if we want to speak of the bread as a metaphor for the dough, we must recognize that a metaphorical transposition has transferred the term "metaphor" out of the realm of rhetoric and into an extra-rhetorical realm. Why then does de Man press this untenable point? Apparently he is attempting to salvage some vestige of his theory that deconstruction arises from the tension between "grammar" and "rhetoric." It would be too obviously silly to suggest explicitly that the genetic principle, the imputed source of trouble in this book, is a metaphor. Then perhaps we can have metaphor and therefore rhetoric resulting from some operation of the genetic principle. But in de Man's use of the word "metaphor" for Apollo, the word "metaphor" no longer has anything to do with rhetoric, and can have no possible relevance to grammar, having been removed from the realm in which "deconstructions" might be conceived to occur. It is therefore inevitable that when de Man introduces explicit reference to his guiding thesis near the end of his final paragraph, he does so only to change the subject and to introduce a new and quite extraordinary logic.

The de Man sentence begins, "Moreover, bearing in mind the analogy that operates, in *The Birth of Tragedy*, between genetic movements in history and semiological relationships in language. . . ." The "analogy" is strictly a creation of de Man's text—Apollo is a metaphor—and there has been no demonstration that it "operates" in *The Birth of Tragedy*. Having created his special meaning of "metaphor," and having done so to achieve an analysis which does not occur, de Man continues the sentence above by saying, "the rhetorically self-conscious reading puts into question the authority of metaphor as a paradigm of poetic language." The new subject is the relationship of metaphor to poetic language generally. In de Man's final sentence he informs us that what he has previously called "metaphor" is actually a "metonymy"—or rather, "a blind metonymy"—and that, mysteriously enough, the realization of this fact in itself achieves deconstruction. De Man says, "For if genetic models are only one instance of rhetorical mystification among others, and if the relationship between the figural and the proper meaning of metaphor is conceived, as in this text, in genetic terms, then metaphor becomes a blind metonymy and the entire set of values that figures so prominently in *The Birth of Tragedy*—a melocentric [meaning "logocentric"] theory of language, the pan-tragic consciousness of the self, and the genetic vision of history—are made to appear hollow when they are exposed to the clarity of a new ironic light."[80] In light of what has been said heretofore, this does not seem to require further comment.

One additional point needs to be made. The terms "genetic" and "logocentrism" have become virtual synonyms in de Man's text. He tells us that Nietzsche's work after *The Birth of Tragedy* "participates in the radical rejection of the genetic teleology associated with Romantic idealism." He says also, "A great number of passages from *The Birth of Tragedy* seem to place the text forcefully within the logocentric tradition. The later evolution of Nietzsche's work could then be understood as the gradual 'deconstruction' of a logocentrism that receives its fullest expression in *The Birth of Tragedy*." And the genetic and logocentrism are inseparable: "The logocentric valorization necessarily implies the persistence of the genetic model as its only possible representation in temporal or hierarchical terms."[81] Clearly the deconstruction of logocentrism in the later work means the deconstruction of the genetic principle. De Man's argument collapses if the genetic principle does not disappear from Nietzsche's later work. One of the most important of commentaries on Nietzsche is Gilles Deleuze's *Nietzsche and Philosophy,* a work that de Man quotes in another context.[82] Deleuze says, "Nietzsche creates the new concept of genealogy. The philosopher is a genealogist rather than a Kantian tribunal judge or a utilitarian mechanic." He says also, "Nietzsche calls the genealogical element of force the will to power. Genealogical means differential and genetic."[83] Deleuze uses the term "genetic" continually in speaking of Nietzsche's mature work, his basic thought. The evidence thus far seems to be clear. Like Derrida, de Man creates fictions in order to deconstruct, but de Man also creates fictions in order to deconstruct them.

Having interrogated de Man's work on its own terms, one may, with some point, ask a larger, simpler, and more obvious question which no one, including de Man, bothered to ask. What could it possibly mean to "deconstruct" a literary text or to find that it "deconstructs itself"? Where Derrida is concerned, a comparable question has a clear answer. Derrida deconstructs individual concepts— "sign," "supplement," "nature," "origin," for instance. The effect of the deconstruction is to invalidate the term. Previously we used the term with little hesitation; now we discard it, or employ it with hesitation or apology. The term drops out of discourse, becomes past history. Its value and status have radically changed. But what happens to the status of a literary text that has been deconstructed?

At this point we will do well to remember something that deconstructionism has served to obscure. For Derrida everything becomes simply a "text." People, physical objects, poems, philosophical dissertations—all are texts, embodiments of language. It would follow—most logically—that the questions we should put to philosophical dissertations are the questions we should put to literary texts and that there is no essential difference. Though this is a very limited part of the truth, in the abstract it may seem a very brilliant observation. For Derrida, who does not deal with literary texts as such, it presents no problem. For de Man's part, we should remember that his treatment of "rhetoric" and "grammar" does not observe the linguistic solipsism which removes the distinctions that are relevant here. In specific application the idea that all things indiscriminately are texts can be disastrous, for the truth remains that literary texts are in one degree or another works of art and they are not philosophical dissertations. The two genres might conceivably be considered the same if we assumed the absolute autonomy of language and its absolute determining power, but in none of de Man's analyses does he make those improbable assumptions. De Man's deconstruction always amounts to discovering logical conflicts or inconsistencies within the literary text. As I have said elsewhere, we do not require of the poet that he be intellectually consistent.[84] The issue of logical consistency in a work of art can be weighed, however, only in the light of specific artistic or literary theories.

Suppose we assume that every work of art is, if not fundamentally, then at least in some significant respect, an imitation of life. Life is persistently inconsistent. Always without logic, we make love; always against logic, we get married. And, alas, does not my life implacably deconstruct itself? As someone has said, we are certain of our deaths and yet most of us live as though we were immortal. Considered as an imitation of life, art is necessarily inconsistent. It has been said that Shakespeare wrote as though there were no God but as though men had souls. I have pointed out that every major poem of Robert Browning contradicts itself in an "antithetical ending," but this has nothing to do with a "tension between grammar and rhetoric" and is a reflection of the faltering incipience of a cultural revolution, an imitation of life.[85] The Kantian aesthetic, in establishing art as a separate ontological order, made the question of its logical consistency totally irrelevant. Claude Lévi-Strauss has said of myth and Burke has said of art that they serve the function of reconciling logical conflicts, and obviously they do that by extralogical means. The logical conflicts are not abolished; they are overcome, and precisely and necessarily by illogical devices. What we require of art is not logic but persuasion. From what conceivable point of view can the question of the logical consistency of art have a significance for which the word "deconstruction" would be appropriate? De Man has said that the kind of study of logical inconsistencies that he has effected in Proust, as fully described above, would be applicable "with proper modifications of technique to Milton or to Dante or to Hölderlin." Then he assures us, "This will in fact be the task of literary criticism in coming years."[86] To what effect? we must ask. Has anyone really ever doubted that logical inconsistencies are to be found in all the great philosophers, let alone all the great poets? Would defining such inconsistencies alter the status of the works of Milton, Dante, or Hölderlin in a way that has not occurred in the historical course of cultural transformation? What is the conception of art that endows with significance what de Man calls "deconstruction"? I do not see how we can escape a conclusion which would otherwise seem improbable—that de Man's theoretical project, which is not coherently sustained in practice, is based upon a fundamental confusion of genres and is thus from its inception quite inane.

notes

Abbreviations Used in Notes

Listed below are the abbreviations used to refer to selected reference items in the notes. Complete bibliographical information is included in the Bibliography.

ATH   Burke, Kenneth. *Attitudes Toward History.*
BT   Heidegger, Martin. *Being and Time.*
BW   Krell, David Farrell, ed. *Martin Heidegger: Basic Writings.*
CS   Burke, Kenneth. *Counter-Statement.*
DT   Heidegger, Martin. *Discourse on Thinking.*
GM   Burke, Kenneth. *A Grammar of Motives.*
IM   Heidegger, Martin. *An Introduction to Metaphysics.*
LSA   Burke, Kenneth. *Language as Symbolic Action.*
N4   Heidegger, Martin. *Nihilism.*
OTB   Heidegger, Martin. *On "Time and Being."*
OWL   Heidegger, Martin. *On the Way to Language.*
PC   Burke, Kenneth. *Permanence and Change.*
PH   Gadamer, Hans-Georg. *Philosophical Hermeneutics.*
PLF   Burke, Kenneth. *The Philosophy of Literary Form.*
PLT   Heidegger, Martin. *Poetry, Language, Thought.*
PSF   Cassirer, Ernst. *The Philosophy of Symbolic Forms.*
QTO   Heidegger, Martin. *The Question Concerning Technology.*
RM   Burke, Kenneth. *A Rhetoric of Motives.*
RR   Burke, Kenneth. *The Rhetoric of Religion.*

133

TM   Gadamer, Hans-Georg. *Truth and Method.*
WCT   Heidegger, Martin. *What Is Called Thinking?*
WP   Nietzsche, Friedrich. *The Will to Power.*

Chapter 1. Introduction

1. Kenneth Burke, "The Rhetoric of Hitler's 'Battle,'" in *The Philosophy of Literary Form,* 3d ed., rev., 191–220. Cited hereafter in the notes as PLF.
2. I am indebted for some biographical details to Timothy Crusius, of Texas A & M University, who has in preparation an excellent general study of Burke.
3. Martin Heidegger, *Being and Time.* Cited hereafter in the notes as BT.
4. Richard Kostelanetz, "A Mind That Cannot Stop Exploding," *New York Times Book Review,* March 15, 1981.
5. Heidegger, *What Is Called Thinking?,* 51, 57, 55, 46. Cited hereafter in the notes as WCT. Wherever a series of sources and/or page numbers appear in a single note, they document in the order in which they appear a series of quotations immediately preceding and including that at which the note number appears in the text.
6. Heidegger, *Nihilism.,* vol. 4 of *Nietzsche,* 147, 136, 257, 133, 140. Cited hereafter in the notes as N4.
7. Burke, *Counter-Statement,* 2d ed., 203. Cited hereafter in the notes as CS.
8. Burke, *Permanence and Change: An Anatomy of Purpose,* 2d ed., 162. Cited hereafter in the notes as PC.
9. Burke, *A Grammar of Motives,* 305. Cited hereafter in the notes as GM.
10. PC, 46.
11. N4, 117.
12. PC, 74.
13. WCT, 29.
14. Heidegger, "Science and Reflection," *The Question Concerning Technology and Other Essays,* 176. Cited hereafter in the notes as QTO.
15. Ernst Cassirer, *The Philosophy of Symbolic Forms,* trans. Ralph Manheim, vol. 3, *The Phenomenology of Knowledge,* 94. Cited hereafter in the notes as PSF.
16. PSF, vol. 2, *Mythical Thought,* 255–56.
17. Burke, "A Dramatistic View of the Origins of Language," *Language as Symbolic Action: Essays on Life, Literature, and Method,* 469. Cited hereafter in the notes as LSA.
18. Burke, *The Rhetoric of Religion: Studies in Logology,* 33. Cited hereafter in the notes as RR.
19. Burke, *A Rhetoric of Motives,* 276. Cited hereafter in the notes as RM.
20. PC, 63.
21. Heidegger, "Letter on Humanism," in David Farrell Krell, ed., *Martin Heidegger: Basic Writings,* 210. Cited hereafter in the notes as BW.

22. Alexander Kojeve, *Introduction to the Reading of Hegel: Lectures on the Phenonology of Spirit*, 258, 259 n41.
23. Frank Lentricchia, *Criticism and Social Change.*

Chapter 2. Common Ground and "Being There"

1. Nelson Goodman, *Ways of Worldmaking*, 6.
2. Friedrich Nietzsche, *The Will to Power*, (506) 275. Here as elsewhere in references to *The Will to Power* the page number will be preceded by the number of the Fragment in parenthesis. Cited hereafter in the notes as WP.
3. Such a dual system is proposed by Allan Paivio, *Imagery and Verbal Processes*, 8.
4. Jan Aler, "Heidegger's Conception of Language in *Being and Time*," in *On Heidegger and Language*, trans. and ed. Joseph J. Kockelmans, 60.
5. Joseph P. Fell, *Heidegger and Sartre: An Essay on Being and Place*, 197. Heinrich Ott says that in the later Heidegger "man is completely determined in his Being by language."—"Hermeneutic and Personal Structure," in *On Heidegger and Language*, ed. Kockelmans, 175.
6. "Letter on Humanism," BW, 206.
7. Heidegger, *An Introduction to Metaphysics*, trans. Manheim, 13. Cited hereafter in the notes as IM.
8. CS, 91.
9. PLF, 83.
10. "Definition of Man," LSA, 19.
11. PSF 3:49.
12. PSF 3:205–77.
13. PSF 3:448.
14. PSF 3:277.
15. Burke, *Attitudes Toward History*, 2d ed., 373. Cited hereafter in the notes as ATH.
16. PC, 168, 168, 235.
17. "Definition of Man," LSA, 11.
18. PC, 168.
19. PC, 35; RR, 272; RM, 136; LSA, 9, 48.
20. "Terministic Screens," LSA, 61.
21. Cassirer, *Language*, vol. 1 of PSF, 178; "Terministic Screens," LSA, 45; "Letter on Humanism," BW, 206; BT, 193 and 89; BT, 195.
22. "Terministic Screens," LSA, 53.
23. BT, 62.
24. PC, 106. See also pp. 152, 153.
25. PC, 25.
26. Burke, "Definition of Man," LSA, 5; "What Are the Signs of What?" LSA, 363; BT, 414; "Semantic and Poetic Meaning," PLF, 159.
27. BT, 241, 428, 194.

28. PC, 271, 163.
29. PC, 271.
30. BT, 448.
31. WP, (585) 317, (487) 269; PSF 3:99, 320, 473.
32. BT, 241; ATH, 68, 68.
33. Hugh Kenner, *The Pound Era*, 153.
34. *Mythical Thought*, vol. 2 of PSF, 88.
35. WP, (462) 255, (1066) 549, (293) 165, (617) 330.
36. WCT, 79, 79.
37. Hans-Georg Gadamer, *Philosophical Hermeneutics*, 156, 152. Cited hereafter in the notes as PH.
38. Gadamer, PH, 152; PSF 3:320, 321; *Truth and Method*, 218. (*Truth and Method* is cited hereafter in the notes as TM.)
39. IM, 105.
40. PH, 184.
41. Ibid., 172.
42. GM, 33.
43. Max Scheler, "Reality and Resistance: On *Being and Time*," in *Heidegger: The Man and Thinker*, ed. Thomas Sheehan, 135.
44. BT, 50.
45. Edmund Husserl, *Ideas: General Introduction to Pure Phenomenology*, 96–100, 151–67.
46. Paul Ricoeur, *Husserl: An Analysis of His Phenomenology*, 31.
47. Husserl, *Cartesian Meditations: An Introduction to Phenomenology*, 89–157.
48. BT, 249.
49. BT, 207.
50. Lovitt cites a letter from Heidegger to J. Glenn Gray of October 10, 1972.—QTO, xxxv n2.
51. Husserl, *Ideas*, 235–59.
52. BT, 416, 209, 207.
53. Heidegger, "The Origin of the Work of Art," *Poetry, Language, Thought*, 52 (cited hereafter in the notes as PLT); BT, 206.
54. Joseph J. Kockelmans says, "Anyone who talks about Heidegger's 'philosophy' with greater clarity and precision than Heidegger misunderstands the genuine meaning of Heidegger's thought and misleads his audience."—"Ontological Difference, Hermeneutics, and Language," in Kockelmans, *On Heidegger and Language*, 228. However, that would mean that Heidegger may not be discussed.
55. BT, 374, 374, 488.
56. TM, 228.
57. BT, 418.
58. *Criticism and Social Change*, 118.
59. BT, 220, 213, 212, 443, 443.
60. BT, 448, 443, 443, 220, 220.
61. BT, 220, 220.

62. BT, 220, 220.
63. BT, 375.
64. BT, 331, 227.
65. BT, 234.
66. BT, 321, 333, 320, 232, 235, 316.
67. BT, 279.
68. BT, 416, 264.
69. BT, 330, 183, 307, 293, 307, 291.
70. BT, 293.
71. BT, 295, 294, 304, 298, 298.
72. BT, 68, 314, 350, 308, 294, 307.
73. BT, 309, 308, 358.
74. BT, 345, 444, 437, 387.
75. WP, (971) 509, (995) 518.
76. WP, 307.
77. WP, (916) 484, (1041) 536.
78. BT, 488.

Chapter 3. Burke's Act and Paradox of Being

1. The reader approaching Burke's work for the first time should begin with *Permanence and Change*, in many ways his most appealing work and essential to all that follows.
2. PC, 163.
3. GM, 505, 505–6.
4. TM, 413–14; PC, 272; PC, 272.
5. An arresting treatment of the relationship between logology and theology is to be found in the epilogue to *The Rhetoric of Religion*, entitled "Prologue in Heaven."
6. RR, 191.
7. RR, 75, 114, 114.
8. Jacques Lacan, *Écrits*, 30–107.
9. ATH, 200, 200; TM, 58; PC, 101, 24; RR, 149; BT, 262; RR, 149, 149–50.
10. PC, 235.
11. PC, 118, 118.
12. GM, 19.
13. GM, 40.
14. Lentricchia, *Criticism and Social Change*, 73, 106, 137.
15. ATH, 184. See also pp. 263–64.
16. GM, xviii; PC, 118; GM, 340, xxiii, xv.
17. GM, xv, xv.
18. GM, 228.
19. GM, 127.

20. GM, 127–29.
21. GM, 15, 11.
22. GM, 444, xix.
23. GM, 127.
24. GM, 127–320.
25. PC, 221.
26. GM, 190.
27. Lentricchia, *Criticism and Social Change*, 68.
28. Ibid., 67.
29. GM, xxiii.
30. *Criticism and Social Change*, 74.
31. Ibid., 71.
32. Ibid., 68.
33. WP, (517) 280; GM, 24, 25.
34. BT, 97–98.
35. BT, 412–15. See also pp. 114–22, 134–48.
36. BT, 413, 487, 487.
37. GM, 24, 56.
38. Fell, *Heidegger and Sartre*, 73, 298.
39. GM, 21, 466, 64, 190, 109, xix.
40. GM, xviii, xv, 317.
41. GM, xxiii, 505–6, 66, 57, 340, 317, 317.

Chapter 4. Being: The Later Heidegger

1. "Letter on Humanism," BW, 193. See also Heidegger, "The Nature of Language," in *On the Way to Language*, 63. Cited hereafter in the notes as OWL. The statement is revised in "Dialogue on Language," OWL, 5.
2. "Dialogue on Language," OWL, 58, 50.
3. "Building Dwelling Thinking," PLT, 146; ". . . Poetically Man Dwells . . ." PLT, 216.
4. "The Nature of Language," OWL, 107, 50.
5. "The Way to Language," OWL, 134.
6. Kenneth Burke has said recently, "I go along with Santayana's brand of metaphysical materialism according to which I have 'animal faith' in the conviction that the world 'out there' is not solipsistically *my* dream, though there is no way of proving it."—Letter to the author, February 29, 1984. It is perhaps unnecessary to say that Burke's animal-faith materialism does not imply that he is a positivist.
7. ATH, 293–98.
8. GM, 305; "Terministic Screens," LSA, 44.
9. Fredric Jameson, *The Prison-House of Language: A Critical Account of Structuralism and Russian Formalism*, 212.

10. "A Dialogue on Language," OWL, 50.
11. Preface to William J. Richardson, *Heidegger: Through Phenomenology to Thought*, xvi. The Preface is a lengthy letter from Heidegger to Richardson.
12. "Dialogue on Language," OWL, 7; WCT, 213, 212; "Letter on Humanism," BW, 242, 235; WCT, 12.
13. IM, 132.
14. PLT, 15–87.
15. "The Origin of the Work of Art," PLT, 57, 45, 39, 71, 86.
16. Ibid., 36, 46.
17. Ibid., 77, 78, 72, 74, 73.
18. RM, 145–46 and 333, for instance.
19. Heidegger, "The End of Philosophy," *On "Time and Being,"* 72. Cited hereafter in the notes as OTB.
20. *An Introduction to Metaphysics* is preparatory to this crucial work.
21. WCT, 85.
22. WCT, 139, 139, 153, 140, 140, 141, 144, 151.
23. WCT, 132, 140, 71, 71; "The Nature of Language," OWL, 83, 69.
24. N4, 141.
25. BT, 255, 269–70, 269.
26. Richardson, *Heidegger*, 240, 259.
27. WCT, 121; "What Are Poets For?" PLT, 101; WCT, 235; "The Turning," QTO, 44; WCT, 41.
28. WCT, 41.
29. IM, 194–95.
30. IM, 122; N4, 217; IM, 133.
31. "Letter on Humanism," BW, 199; IM, 163; WCT, 62, 180.
32. "The Question Concerning Technology," QTO, 19; "The Turning," QTO, 37, 37, 37, 43, 38, 39, 39, 44, 44–45, 47.
33. "The Turning," QTO, 47.
34. WCT, 79.
35. IM, 124, 130, 134, 138, 138, 175, 205, 185.
36. IM, 51, 53.
37. "Language," PLT, 189.
38. "The Way to Language," OWL, 124, 124, 122–23, 126; "Words," OWL, 155; "Letter on Humanism," BW, 206; "The Way to Language," OWL, 126.
39. Heidegger, "Memorial Address," *Discourse on Thinking*, 55. Cited hereafter in the notes as DT.
40. "Time and Being," OTB, 2.
41. Ibid., 3, 19.
42. Ibid., 19
43. OTB, 2. Otto Pöggeler, in his article "Seins als Ereignis," says that in "Time and Being" "Heidegger reaches the goal he set before himself in *BT*."— Quoted by J. L. Mehta, *Martin Heidegger: The Way and the Vision*, rev. ed., 473 n30. Mehta says that his own interpretation is "not quite the equivalent" of Pöggeler's. See Mehta, 463–69.

44. "The Way to Language," OWL, 127; "Time and Being," OTB, 17.
45. "Time and Being," OTB, 20.
46. Ibid., 22.
47. Ibid., 23.
48. Ibid.
49. Ibid.
50. Ibid., 24, 24.
51. "Time and Being," OTB, 24, 24; "The End of Philosophy and the Task of Thinking," OTB, 58, 59, 60, 60.
52. "The End of Philosophy," OTB, 73.
53. Jacques Derrida, *Of Grammatology*, 19.
54. Heidegger, "The Question of Being," *The Question of Being*, 71, 81.
55. *Of Grammatology*, 23.
56. BT, 63.
57. Vincent B. Leitch, *Deconstructive Criticism: An Advanced Introduction*, 70.

Chapter 5. The "Thing" and Questions of Faith

1. "Building Dwelling Thinking," PLT, 150, 149; "The Word of Nietzsche: 'God Is Dead'," QTO, 100, 69; "Building Dwelling Thinking," PLT, 153; QTO, 69; "Memorial Address," DT, 48.
2. BT, 465.
3. "Building Dwelling Thinking," PLT, 153.
4. "The Thing," PLT, 172.
5. Ibid.
6. Ibid., 173.
7. "Language," PLT, 202; "The Thing," PLT, 171; IM, 16.
8. IM, 14.
9. IM, 45; "The Thing," PLT, 179.
10. Fell, *Heidegger and Sartre*, 397. See also p. 414.
11. Fell, *Heidegger and Sartre*, 231; BT, 89; "The Nature of Language," OWL, 62; Fell, *Heidegger and Sartre*, 231; "Origins of Language," LSA, 429; Fell, *Heidegger and Sartre*, 255, 262; GM, 24.
12. "The Origin of the Work of Art," PLT, 47, 47, 46; PH, 223.
13. Fell, *Heidegger and Sartre*, 47, 195–96.
14. "The Turning," QTO, 42, 40, 40, 42, 41, 41, 42.
15. GM, 56.
16. "An Account of the Four Essays," in *Existence and Being*, 186.
17. In Kockelmans, ed., "Panel Discussion," *On Heidegger and Language*, 190.
18. John Macquarrie, *Martin Heidegger*, 59. George Steiner's statement that it is possible to substitute the word "God" wherever Heidegger says "Being" is misleading.—George Steiner, *Martin Heidegger*, 155–56.
19. David Farrell Krell, "General Introduction: 'The Question of Being'," BW, 32–33.

20. Richardson, *Heidegger,* 679 n4.
21. PC, 246.
22. "The Turning," QTO, 39.
23. Ibid., 47.
24. Ibid.
25. WCT, 177. See also N4, 248.
26. Richardson, *Heidegger,* 640. Richardson also speculates, perhaps hopefully, on a "Ur-Heidegger" (pp. 628–33), presumably a Heidegger more religious than the Heidegger revealed in his texts.
27. "'Only a God Can Save Us': The *Spiegel* Interview (1966)," in Sheehan, *Heidegger,* 57.
28. PC, 272. See also "Definition of Man" and "Terministic Screens," LSA, 5, 48.
29. BT, 223. See also IM, 110, 113.
30. "What Are Poets For?" PLT, 92.
31. RM, 180, 289.
32. Pierre Teilhard de Chardin, *The Phenomenon of Man.*
33. GM, 152–58.
34. GM, 154–58.
35. GM, 154, 157, 154.
36. RM, 331, 331, 332.
37. RM, 332, 332.
38. RM, 333.
39. Ibid.
40. "The Turning," QTO, 49.
41. BW, 95–112.
42. "What is Metaphysics?" BW, 98, 99, 107.
43. Ibid., 102, 101, 104, 108, 108, 105, 111, 110.
44. Reprinted together with "Post Scripts on the Negative," LSA, 419–79.
45. LSA, 422–24.
46. LSA, 478.
47. LSA, 469, 419, 420.
48. Fell, *Heidegger and Sartre,* 165.
49. LSA, 454, 454, 454, 454, 454–55, 459, 454.
50. LSA, 455.
51. LSA, 456.
52. RR, 21.
53. Ibid.
54. Ibid.

Chapter 6. Conclusion

1. Theodor W. Adorno, *The Jargon of Authenticity,* 121.
2. GM, 248.

3. Poem entitled "When the early morning light quietly / grows above the mountains . . ." (PLT, 4).

4. Richard Rorty, *Philosophy and the Mirror of Nature*.

5. Robert Nozick, *Philosophical Explanations*, 2.

6. "Memorial Address," DT, 55.

7. "Definition of Man," LSA, 21.

8. *Of Grammatology*, 158.

9. *Criticism and Social Change*, 19.

10. The political import of this book is clear. In a "destructive poetics" we sing our hearts out for total destruction. Neither Lentricchia nor Marx participates in such extremism.

11. Bové's article is "The Ineluctability of Difference: Scientific Pluralism and the Critical Intelligence," *Boundary-2*, Fall 1983, 155–69.

12. *The Jargon of Authenticity*, 122.

13. BT, 262. Quoted in *Destructive Poetics*, 55.

14. *Destructive Poetics*, 69.

15. Ibid., 91, 92, 92. The crucial shift of meaning that results from Bové's shift of emphasis is clearly illustrated in his treatment of Heidegger's "retrieve" as interpretation. Heidegger says, "This means nothing less than to re-trieve the beginning of our historical-spiritual Dasein in order to transmute it into another beginning."—IM, 39. For Bové this means "to *displace* that beginning and to establish *another*" [my italics].—*Destructive Poetics*, 88.

16. *Criticism and Social Change*, 76, 19, 71.

17. BW, 181, 183.

18. PLF, 23.

19. PLF, 61; ATH, 184.

Appendix: Note Against Deconstructionism

1. *Of Grammatology*, 52.

2. Ibid., 4, 6.

3. Ibid., 8.

4. Ibid., 93.

5. Ibid., 12; Derrida, "Structure, Sign and Play in the Discourse of the Human Sciences," in *Writing and Difference*, 279; *Of Grammatology*, 70, 65, 69, 40–41.

6. *Of Grammatology*, 163, 158. The French is "*il n'y a pas de hors-texts*," which, as the translator indicates, would be literally "there is no outside-text"; but that is only a more rigorously Derridean way of saying, "There is nothing outside of the text."

7. Ibid., 73, 13.

8. Ibid., 49.

9. Ibid., 50.

10. WP, (699) 371.

11. Derrida, *Positions*, 41.
12. Derrida, *Margins of Philosophy*, 329.
13. *Positions*, 6.
14. Ibid.
15. *Of Grammatology*, 29–73.
16. Ibid., 31.
17. Ibid., 43.
18. Ibid., 57.
19. Ibid.
20. Ibid., 56.
21. Ibid., 238.
22. Ibid., 44.
23. Ibid., 55, 87.
24. Ibid., 92.
25. Jonathan Culler, *On Deconstruction: Theory and Criticism after Structuralism*, 96; *Of Grammatology*, 73, 75, 75, 65, 47.
26. *Of Grammatology*, 57, 166, 68; *Positions*, 26; *Speech and Phenomena: And Other Essays on Husserl's Theory of Signs*, 129–60, 138, 130, 147, 152, 153; *Of Grammatology*, 62, 268.
27. *Of Grammatology*, 26, 49.
28. *Of Grammatology*, 40–41, 53, 44, 44.
29. *Positions*, 55; *Of Grammatology*, 22, 22–23.
30. *Of Grammatology*, 57, 59, 61.
31. *Of Grammatology*, 60, 60, 60, 60, 61, 61.
32. *Of Grammatology*, 61, 61, 61.
33. *Positions*, 26.
34. De Man, *Allegories of Reading: Figural Language in Rousseau, Nietzsche, Rilke, and Proust*.
35. Ibid., 10, 17, 18, 19.
36. Ibid., 18, 18.
37. Ibid., 7.
38. Ibid., 8, 6.
39. Ibid., 9.
40. Ibid., 9, 9.
41. Ibid., 12, 15, 12, 12, 12, 12.
42. Ibid., 6, 6.
43. Ibid., 5, 5.
44. Ibid., 12.
45. Ibid., 13, 13.
46. Ibid., 16.
47. Ibid., 61, 62.
48. Ibid., 99, 82, 82.
49. Ibid., 79, 79, 80, 82, 82.
50. Nietzsche, *The Birth of Tragedy* and *The Case of Wagner*, 13.
51. Ibid., 36.

52. Ibid., 52.
53. Ibid., 33, 33, 96, 94.
54. Ibid., "Attempt at Self-Criticism," *The Birth of Tragedy*, 19, 24, 24.
55. *Allegories of Reading*, 84.
56. *The Birth of Tragedy*, 33.
57. Ibid., 33, 99, 45, 47, 66, 47, 128, 33, 140, 143–44, 66; *Allegories of Reading*, 85.
58. *The Birth of Tragedy*, 119.
59. *Allegories of Reading*, 84, 84, 85, 86, 87, 85, 85, 86, 87.
60. Ibid., 87.
61. *The Birth of Tragedy*, 102; *Allegories of Reading*,, 96, 96, 96, 96; *The Birth of Tragedy*, 48, 52.
62. *Allegories of Reading*, 98.
63. *The Birth of Tragedy*, 109–110; *Allegories of Reading*, 99; *The Birth of Tragedy*, 110, 104, 104; *Allegories of Reading*, 96; *The Birth of Tragedy*, 61.
64. *Allegories of Reading*, 94, 100.
65. Ibid., 100.
66. Ibid., 101, 101, 100–101.
67. Ibid., 99; *The Birth of Tragedy*, 141, 46, 46–47, 71, 49; *Allegories of Reading*, 99.
68. *Allegories of Reading*, 81, 88, 88.
69. Ibid., 88.
70. *The Birth of Tragedy*, 55–56.
71. Ibid., 103, 105; *Allegories of Reading*, 88, 88, 88.
72. *Allegories of Reading*, 87, 98, 99.
73. Ibid., 98.
74. Ibid., 83, 85.
75. Ibid., 93.
76. *The Birth of Tragedy*, 126.
77. *Allegories of Reading*, 97–98, 98.
78. *The Birth of Tragedy*, 67.
79. *Allegories of Reading*, 91.
80. Ibid., 102, 102.
81. Ibid., 82, 88, 88.
82. Gilles Deleuze, *Nietzsche and Philosophy*.
83. Ibid., 2, 52.
84. Samuel B. Southwell, *Quest for Eros: Browning and "Fifine,"* 101.
85. Ibid., 209, 214, 220, 231.
86. *Allegories of Reading*, 16–17.

bibliography

Adorno, Theodor W. *The Jargon of Authenticity.* Translated by Knut Tarnowski and Frederic Will. Evanston, Ill.: Northwestern University Press, 1973.

Aronowitz, Stanley. *The Crisis in Historical Materialism: Class, Politics and Culture in Marxist Thought.* New York: Praeger Publishers, 1981.

Bové, Paul. *Destructive Poetics: Heidegger and Modern Poetry.* New York: Columbia University Press, 1980.

―――. "The Ineluctability of Difference: Scientific Pluralism and the Critical Intelligence." *Boundary-2,* Fall 1983, 155–69.

Burke, Kenneth. *Attitudes toward History.* 1959. 2d ed. Boston: Beacon Press, 1961.

―――. *Counter-Statement.* 1953. 2d ed. Berkeley and Los Angeles: University of California Press, 1968.

―――. *A Grammar of Motives.* 1945. Reprint. Berkeley and Los Angeles: Univeristy of California Press, 1969.

―――. *Language as Symbolic Action: Essays on Life, Literature, and Method.* Berkeley and Los Angeles: University of California Press, 1966.

―――. *Permanence and Change: An Anatomy of Purpose.* 2d ed. Indianapolis, Indiana: The Bobbs-Merrill Company, Inc., 1954.

―――. *The Philosophy of Literary Form.* 3d ed. Berkeley and Los Angeles: University of California Press, 1973.

―――. *A Rhetoric of Motives.* 1950. Reprint. Berkeley and Los Angeles: University of California Press, 1969.

―――. *The Rhetoric of Religion: Studies in Logology.* 1961. Reprint. Berkeley and Los Angeles: University of California Press, 1970.

145

Cassirer, Ernst. *The Philosophy of Symbolic Forms*. Translated by Ralph Manheim. 3 vols. New Haven and London: Yale University Press, 1957.

Chardin, Pierre Teilhard de. *The Phenomenon of Man*. Translated by Bernard Wall. New York: Harper and Brothers Publishers, 1959.

Culler, Jonathan. *On Deconstruction: Theory and Criticism After Structuralism*. Ithaca, N.Y.: Cornell University Press, 1982.

Deleuze, Gilles. *Nietzsche and Philosophy*. Translated by Hugh Tomlinson. New York: Columbia University Press, 1983.

De Man, Paul. *Allegories of Reading: Figural Language in Rousseau, Nietzsche, Rilke, and Proust*. New Haven and London: Yale University Press, 1979.

Derrida, Jacques. *Of Grammatology*. Translated by Gayatri Chakravorty Spivak. Baltimore and London: Johns Hopkins University Press, 1976.

———. *Margins of Philosophy*. Translated by Alan Bass. Chicago: University of Chicago Press, 1982.

———. *Positions*. Translated by Alan Bass. Chicago: The University of Chicago Press, 1981.

———. *Speech and Phenomena: And Other Essays on Husserl's Theory of Signs*. Translated by David B. Allison. Evanston, Ill.: Northwestern University Press, 1973.

———. *Writing and Difference*. Translated by Alan Bass. Chicago: The University of Chicago Press, 1978.

Fell, Joseph P. *Heidegger and Sartre: An Essay on Being and Place*. New York: Columbia University Press, 1979.

Gadamer, Hans-Georg. *Philosophical Hermeneutics*. Translated and edited by David E. Linge. Berkeley and Los Angeles: University of California Press, 1976.

———. *Truth and Method*. Translator not indicated. New York: The Crossroad Publishing Company, 1975.

Goodman, Nelson. *Ways of Worldmaking*. Indianapolis and Cambridge: Hackett Publishing Company, 1978.

Heidegger, Martin. *Basic Writings*. Edited by David Farrell Krell. New York: Harper and Row, Publishers, 1977.

———. *Being and Time*. Translated by John Macquarrie and Edward Robinson. New York: Harper and Row, Publishers, 1962.

———. *Discourse on Thinking*. Translated by John M. Anderson and E. Hans Freund. New York: Harper and Row, Publishers, 1966.

———. *Existence and Being*. Translated by Stefan Schimanski. South Bend, Ind.: Regnery/Gateway, Inc., 1979.

———. *An Introduction to Metaphysics*. Translated by Ralph Manheim. New Haven and London: Yale University Press, 1959.

———. *Nihilism*. Translated by Frank A Capuzzi. Edited by David Farrell Krell. Vol. 4 of *Nietzsche*. New York: Harper and Row, Publishers, 1982.

———. *On the Way to Language*. Translated by Peter D. Hertz. New York: Harper and Row, Publishers, 1971.

———. On "Time and Being." Translated by Joan Stambaugh. New York: Harper and Row, Publishers, 1972.

———. Poetry, Language, Thought. Translated by Albert Hofstadter. New York: Harper and Row, Publishers, 1971.

———. The Question Concerning Technology and Other Essays. Translated and compiled by William Lovitt. New York: Harper and Row, Publishers, 1977.

———. The Question of Being. Translated by William Kluback and Jean T. Wilde. New York: Twayne Publishers, Inc., 1958.

———. What Is Called Thinking? Translated by J. Glenn Gray. New York: Harper and Row, Publishers, 1968.

Husserl, Edmund. Cartesian Meditations: An Introduction to Phenomenology. Translated by Dorion Cairns. The Hague: Martinus Nijhoff, 1977.

———. Ideas: General Introduction to Pure Phenomenology. Translated by W. R. Boyce Gibson. New York: Collier Books; London: Collier Macmillan Publishers, 1962.

Jameson, Fredric. The Prison-House of Language: A Critical Account of Structuralism and Russian Formalism. Princeton, N.J.: Princeton University Press, 1972.

Kenner, Hugh. The Pound Era. Berkeley and Los Angeles: University of California Press, 1971.

Kockelmans, Joseph, ed. and trans. On Heidegger and Language. Evanston, Ill.: Northwestern University Press, 1972.

Kojeve, Alexander. Introduction to the Reading of Hegel: Lectures on the Phenonology of Spirit. Translated by James H. Nichols, Jr. Edited by Allan Bloom. New York: Basic Books, 1969.

Kostelanetz, Richard. "A Mind that Cannot Stop Exploding." New York Times Book Review, March 15, 1981.

Lacan, Jacques. Écrits. Translated by Alan Sheridan. New York: W. W. Norton and Company, Inc., 1977.

Leitch, Vincent B. Deconstructive Criticism: An Advanced Introduction. New York: Columbia University Press, 1983.

Lentricchia, Frank. After the New Criticism. Chicago: University of Chicago Press, 1980.

———. Criticism and Social Change. Chicago: University of Chicago Press, 1983.

Macquarrie, John. Martin Heidegger. Atlanta, Ga.: John Knox Press, 1968.

Mehta, J. L. Martin Heidegger: The Way and the Vision. rev. ed. Honolulu: University Press of Hawaii, 1976.

Nietzsche, Friedrich. The Birth of Tragedy and The Case of Wagner. Translated and edited by Walter Kaufman. New York: Vintage Books, 1967.

———. The Will to Power. Translated by Walter Kaufmann and R. J. Hollingdale. New York: Vintage Books, 1967.

Nozick, Robert. Philosophical Explanations. Cambridge, Mass.: The Belknap Press of Harvard University Press, 1981.

Pavio, Allan. Imagery and Verbal Processes. Hillsdale, N.J. : Lawrence Erlbaum Associates, Publishers, 1979.

Richardson, William J. *Heidegger: Through Phenomenology to Thought.* The Hague: Martinus Nijhoff, 1963.

Ricoeur, Paul. *Husserl: An Analysis of His Phenomenology.* Translated by Edward G. Ballard and Lester E. Embree. Evanston, Ill.: Northwestern University Press, 1967.

Rorty, Richard. *Philosophy and the Mirror of Nature.* Princeton, N.J.: Princeton University Press, 1979.

Sheehan, Thomas, ed. *Heidegger: The Man and the Thinker.* Chicago: Precedent Publishing, Inc., 1981.

Southwell, Samuel B. *Quest for Eros: Browning and "Fifine."* Lexington, Ky.: University Press of Kentucky, 1980.

Steiner, George. *Martin Heidegger.* New York: Penguin Books, 1978.

index

Abyss, 4, 16, 65
Academia: challenged, 86; neurosis of, 76
Accidents, 75
Act: affects history, 36; a *causa sui*, 40; center of knowledge, 32; central to being, 30; creative, 31; escapes knowledge, 31; falsified by analysis, 84; form as alienation of, 50; is free, 31; in Heidegger, 59; illocutionary, 107; infinite components of, 31; and motivation, 33; perlocutionary, 107; pivotal for Burke, 14, 33; transcends language, 32
Adorno, Theodore W., 74, 79
Advent, prayer for, 65
Aesthetic: analysis of, 85; and education, 84–86; and organism, 85; and value, 85
Alienation, cosmic, 75
Ambiguity, valorization of, 57
Analysis, is dismemberment, 79
Animals, as automata, 11
Antithetical ending, 131

Anxiety (*Angst*), 25; social explanation of, 71
Apocalypse, and deconstructionism, 77
Apollonian, 115–29 passim; as falsehood, 121; as metaphor, 127
Appropriation, 54–56
Aquinas, Saint Thomas, 35
Arche-writing, 94–96
Aristotle, 35, 45, 69
Arnold, Matthew, 84
Aronowitz, Stanley: *The Crisis in Historical Materialism*, 78
Art: for art's sake, 78; and being, 45; continuous with life, 46; depends on leap, 46; is essentially poetry, 46; as foundational activity, 46; as guide to reality, 5; as imitation of life, 130; inconsistency of, 131; material emerges in, 62; as origin of art work, 45; is persuasion, 131; reconciles conflicts, 131
Augustine, Saint: *Confessions*, 30–31
Austin, J. L., 107

149

Authenticity, 20, 25, 26, 27, 64, 74
Autonomy, 67

Bakhtin, Mikhail, 2
Being: that ancient something, 56; as
  appearing, 20; autonomy of, 49, 73;
  basis of, in symbolism, 29; as beings, 54, 55; as compromise, 62;
  concepts aligned with, 17; counterpole of movement, 17; of Dasein,
  24–28; and deconstructionism, 76;
  as dependent, 49; destinying of, 56,
  63; and entities, 17; failure to think,
  56; and faith, 65; as foundation of
  meaning, 7; and God, 7, 49;
  Heidegger's project, 5; initiative of,
  49, 50, 64; and a leap, 49; necessary to thought, 17; new grounds
  for, 7; is not time, 54; power over
  man, 50; as present-at-hand, 38;
  requires a place, 50; shepherd of,
  63; *sous rature*, 56–57; as structure
  of becoming, 17–18; thinking anew,
  60; the thinking of, 48–56
Bell, Daniel, 2
Benediction, 68
Bentham, Jeremy, 87
Berkeley, Bishop George, 35, 92
Body, as constant, 6
Bové, Paul, 77, 80; and Derrida, 81;
  Destructive Poetics, 67, 80; emphasis
  by, distorts, 80
Brock, Werner, 64
Browning, Robert, 131
Burke, Kenneth: and abyss, 65, 66;
  accessibility of, 76; accomplishment
  of, 1, 3, 83, 86; aesthetic emphasis
  of, 84–86; and animal faith, 138n6;
  and art, 131; and being in the
  world, 75; and the body, 6; and
  Cassirer, 12–13; challenges academia, 86; contemporaneity of, 81;
  deconstructing act in work of, 81;
  deconstructing philosophy in work
  of, 35; economy of means of, 75;
  embraces all knowledge, 83; five

philosophical languages of, 34; and
  formal grounding, 39; and forms of
  thought, 39; and Gramsci, 81; on
  inconclusiveness, 12; and language,
  44, 72, 73; Lentricchia appropriates, 77, 81; life-world vocabularies
  of, 43, 74; on literature in world,
  77; and Marxism, 82; and material
  world, 43; *Mein Kampf,* warned
  against, 3; and metabiology, 13; and
  metaphysics, 40, 41, 71; and modern thought, 32; and mysticism,
  64–72 passim; and New Criticism,
  4; and new meanings, 30; and
  Nietzsche, 6; and nihilism, 6, 72;
  and politics, 41; and positivism, 65;
  and postmodernism, 85; and reality,
  43; and Romanticism, 85; and
  skeptical grounding, 32; and theoretical knowledge, 38; validifies science, 74; values of, 6; mentioned
  passim
—and Heidegger: on act, 59; and
  causal hypothesis, 12–15; complementary, 82; focal contrast of, 74;
  on grounding of world, 68; gulf
  separating, 73; hermeneutics of, 15,
  82; and Kantian aesthetic, 46; in
  larger perspective, 73–75; on modern age, ending of, 64; mysticism,
  charges of, 7–8; mysticism, question of, 64–72; on National Socialism, 3; and Nietzsche, common
  profile with, 4–6; Nietzsche influenced, 4–6; and paradox of substance, 37–38; and pentad, 36–37,
  61–62; polar relationship of, 74;
  projects of, 18–19; relevance of, to
  literature, 76; styles of, 8–9; superficial similarities of, 3–4; and terministic screens, 15; their theories
  distinctive, 18; and they-world, 30;
  on time, 24–25; on truth, 32
—works of: *Attitudes toward History,*
  43; *Counter-Statement,* 6; "Definition of Man," 76; "A Dramatistic

View of the Origins of Language,"
70; *A Grammar of Motives*, 67,
32–41 passim; *Permanence and
Change*, 29, 32; *A Rhetoric of Motives*, 66, 68; *The Rhetoric of Religion*, 30, 35, 69, 71; "Terministic
Screens," 15

Care, as Dasein's being, 26
Cartesian dream, 76
Cassirer, Ernst, 7, 12–13, 17; on life-
world, 19; parallels with Burke, 3;
serves heuristic purpose, 3
Categories, confusion of, 128
Causal hypothesis, 10–11, 46
Causal thinking, 14
Certainty, Cartesian dream of, 76
Chardin, Pierre Teilhard de, 66
Civilization: cowers, 79;. now begin-
ning, 56
Clough, Arthur, 2
Consciousness: anti-Cartesian rejec-
tion of, 90; artistic activity of, 46;
call of, 26; deconstruction of, 90;
an effect of language, 11; as
nothingness, 70; as unitary, 4
Copenhagen School, 101, 102
Corresponding, 65; as noncausal,
51–52
Creation, as paradigm of act, 32
Criticism: and art, 86; becomes phi-
losophy, 79; becoming deconstruc-
tion, 131; intrinsic and extrinsic,
110–11; requires being, 80
Culler, Jonathan, 97
Culture: as consciousness, 15; at edge
of abyss, 65; and language, 15; lie
of, 121; as product of language, 13

Dante Alighieri, 131
Darwin, Charles, 35, 67
Darwinism, 75
Dasein: as being in the world, 20;
being of, 24–28; forestructure of,
15; as a hermeneutic, 15; its hero,
80; historicality of, 16; meaning of,

23–24; temporality of, 25; is the
world, 23
Death: embrace of, 75; and enframing, 51; individualizes, 27; nuclear,
78; as ownmost possibility, 26–27
Deconstruction: in Burke, 44; of
Christian myth, 69
Deconstructionism: assumptions of,
77; clarifies alternatives, 80; and
consistency, 79; denies referentiality, 96; exclusive legitimacy
of, 88; as fantasy of power, 79; heir
of New Criticism, 77; in ideal
realm, 96; and language, aspects of,
89; mythic tools of, 88; nourishes
apocalypse, 77; an obligation, 93; a
polemical device, 93; rejects being,
76–77; and resentment, 79
Deleuze, Gilles: *Nietzsche and Philosophy*, 129
De Man, Paul, 78; admits theory fails,
108; *Allegories of Reading*, 105–31
passim; changes subject, 128; coherent argument of, 125; confuses
categories, 128; confuses genres,
130, 131; defects in foundations of,
105; discounts logic, 117; and figurative language, 114; logic, strict
in, 114; misreading, his, 121; and
mystery, cultivation of, 123; practice of, incoherent, 131; thesis of,
105
Derrida, Jacques, 40, 56–57; and
being, 2; conceptual world of, 98;
condemns Husserl, 99; creates ideal
realm, 96; *Glas*, 57; and Heidegger,
100; and Hjelmlev, 100; Husserl,
invocation of, 102; logic, immune
to, 103; logocentrism, remains in,
93; *Of Grammatology*, 87–99 passim; *Positions*, 100; and presence,
90; prose of, 89; and solipsism, 91;
sources of, 99; system, outer limit
of, 104; theory of, 90
Descartes, René, 11, 22
Destinying, 50; of Being, 51

Dewey, John, 35
Dialectic, 7; generates Genesis, 30;
    generates philosophy, 35
Dichotomy, deconstructionism im-
    poses, 77
Differance, 98–99
Difference, 98
Dionysian principles, 115–29 passim;
    and falsehood, 120–21
Discourse, 12, 95
Dissonance, semantic, 114; theory of,
    122
Divinities, 58–59
Doric style, 116
Dramatism, 76; culminates in being,
    14; is logology, 30; is terministic
    screen, 15

Earth, 58; art, emerges in, 62;
    grounding of world, 68; and
    noumenon, 63
Ecstasy, mystic, 68
Ego weakness, 79
Einstein, Albert, 17, 75
Eliot, T. S.: *Knowledge and Experience
    in the Philosophy of F. H. Bradley*,
    14–15
Emanation, 50
Enframing (*Gestell*), 51; begins with
    Plato, 64; parallel with death, 51
Equipment (*das Zeug*), 46; as ready-
    to-hand, 37–38; and usefulness, 62
Equiprimordiality, 12
Ersatzmystiken, 68
Eternal recurrence, 18
Event (*Ereignis*), 54; turns on act, 59
Existentialism, 67
Extra-human ground, 66, 75

Fallenness, 25
Fell, Joseph P., 12, 61
Figurative language, duplicity of, 109
Finitude, 27; in Burke, 84; in Heideg-
    ger, 6

Foucault, Michel, 114
Fourfold, the, 42, 58–63; and Aris-
    totle, 61; developed poetically, 60;
    and paradox of substance, 62; and
    pentad, 61–62; in pre-Socratic cul-
    ture, 60–61; in the thing, 60
Freedom, 13, 15
Free play, 79
Freud, Sigmund, 35; Burke's revision
    of, 31; *The Interpretation of Dreams*,
    89
Freudianism, 83

Gadamer, Hans-Georg, 31, 63; elabo-
    rates Heidegger, 3; on life-world,
    19; parallels to Burke, 3; on time as
    being, 24
Gathering, 47, 48, 59
Genetic principle, 114–29 passim;
    and logocentrism, 123; becomes
    rhetoric, 119
Genres, confusion of, 130, 131
Glossematics, 100, 102
Gnosticism, 85, 86
God, 64, 69; and being, 140n18;
    empty place of, 58; as free act, 32
Goodman, Nelson, 10
Grammar: as literal language, 108;
    referentiality implicit in, 106; and
    rhetoric, 107–8
Grammatology: as antigrammar, 88;
    difficulties of, 96; as historical ne-
    cessity, 88; as plurivocity, 95; rele-
    vant as curiosity, 105; supplants
    philosophy, 101; supplants truth,
    88; a tour de force, 99
Gramsci, Antonio, 81
Guilt, 26

Habermas, Jürgen, 2
Hegel, G. W. F., 35, 36, 49; Burke in-
    debted to, 8; called atheist, 8; first
    thinker of writing, 99; and struc-
    ture of becoming, 18

Heidegger, Martin: abandons discursive thought, 56; and arche-writing, 57; assistant to Husserl, 4; called deconstructionist, 80; canonized for failure, 56; dangers in later, 44; and faith, 65; and German Idealism, 74; the later, 44–57; method of, 21; mumbling of, 95; and mysticism, 64–72 passim; and New Criticism, 83; and the past, 80; and representative thinking, 22; style of, 57; mentioned passim. *See also* Burke,—and Heidegger
—works: *Being and Time,* 4, 5, 9, 23–28, 44, 45, 80, passim; "Building Dwelling Thinking," 58, 59; *Discourse on Thinking,* 59; "The End of Philosophy and the Task of Thinking," 56; "Memorial Address," 59; "The Origin of the Work of Art," 45; "The Question Concerning Technology," 51; "The Thing," 58, 59; "Time and Being," 54, 55; "The Turning," 51, 56, 59, 64, 69; "The Way to Language," 55; *What Is Called Thinking?,* 47; "What Is Metaphysics?", 69–72
Hermeneutic circle, 15
Hermeneutics, 4, 80
Hierarchical oppositions, 104
Hierarchy, 69, 93; implicit in Being, 50
Historicism, 25; rejected, 16
History, and choice, 86
Hjelmslev, Louis, 99, 100–101
Hobbes, Thomas, 35
Hölderlin, Friedrich, 131
Hume, David, 35, 87
Husserl, Edmund, 4, 21, 90; *Cartesian Meditations,* 22, 103; Derrida condemns, 99, 103; *Ideas I,* 21; *Ideas II,* 19; reduction of, 101–3

Inconclusiveness, 84

James, William, 35
Johnson, Dr. Samuel, 92

Kant, Immanuel, 10, 35, 63; and Burke's structures, 36; and imagination, 45
Kantian aesthetic, 45, 78, 85, 131; Heidegger close to, 83
Keeping, 47
Kierkegaardian leap, 45, 49
Knowledge, consolidation of, 2
Kropotkin, Prince Peter, 2

Lacan, Jacques, 3, 31
Language: as accident, 75; alienation of, from myth, 124; appropriates us, 42; autonomy of, 2; based on nothing, 81; beginning of, 70; can critique itself, 44; cause of consciousness, 11; centrality of, 10; characteristics of, 89; conceals and unconceals, 15; controls all perspective, 43; as culture, 15; a danger for species, 75; grounded in transcendent, 71; homologies of, with religion, 7; "house of Being," 42; as human faculty, 42, 43; and human world, 13; ignorance of, 89; ineffable, 42; as intellectual impulse, 13; and Kant's transcendentals, 40; as master of man, 42; and music, 124; not an object, 43; not only reality, 86; not supernatural, 68; opens to history, 40; and phenomenology, 15; power of, 4; as prison-house, 43; as pure form, 101; universe made of, 91
Leap, 49
Leibniz, Baron Gottfried Wilhelm, 35, 52
Lentricchia, Frank, 9, 36, 80; *After the New Criticism,* 77; on Burke's act, 33; on Burke's structuralism, 35, 36; *Criticism and Social Change,* 9,

Lentricchia, Frank (*continued*)
  77; criticizes pentad, 36; Neo-
  Marxist position of, 81
Lévi-Strauss, Claude, 131
Life-world, 19–21; necessity of, 37;
  product of language, 43
Literature: not philosophy, 130; re-
  turned to isolation, 81
Locke, John, 35, 87
Logocentrism: the beyond of, 103; the
  breaching of, 95; an error of the
  West, 94; fosters being, 90; and
  metaphysics, 90; and Nietzsche,
  125–26
Logology, 30, 71; and theology, 137 n5
Logos: as language, 53; as original
  oneness, 52; as saying, 53
Luria, A. R., 92

Macquarrie, John, 64
Mallarmé, Stéphane, 95
Man: autonomy of, 67; the shepherd
  of being, 63; *sub specie aeternitatis,*
  29; as symbol user, 14, 71
Marx, Karl, 35, 47
Marxism, 83; of Lentricchia, 78; a
  philosophy of being, 82; revision by
  Burke, 82
Meaning, and visual stimulus, 11
Meaning-beings, 61
Memory, 47, 48; two systems of, 11
Metaphor: applied to things, 106; a
  blind metonymy, 129; inside/out-
  side, 110–11; in Nietzsche,
  126–29; poetic paradigm, 128; as
  related to words, 128; as type of
  combination, 109
Metaphysics: of Aristotle, 69; need for
  new, 5; as representative thinking,
  45; of subjectivity, 5
Mill, John Stuart, 87
Milton, John, 131
Modern age, end of, 64
Modernism, 2

Moment of vision, 28
Monads, 52
Music, and myth, 124
Mysticism, 50; authentic and inauthentic, 68; has neurological basis,
  68; nontheistic, 8, 68; in pure state,
  68; secular analogues of, 68;
  theistic, 8; yields secular truth, 72
Myth, 66; in deconstructionism, 79;
  the existentialist, 67; power of, 126;
  as structure, 17

Narrator, 106
National Socialism. *See* Burke,—and
  Heidegger
Natural selection, 67, 75
Nature, and language, 66
Negative, 69, 70
New Criticism, 4, 77
Newton, Sir Isaac, 17, 75
Nietzsche, Friedrich, 36, 47, 87, 99;
  and *Being and Time,* 28; *The Birth of
  Tragedy,* 114–29; and causal hy-
  pothesis, 10; charged with deceit,
  126; criticized *Birth of Tragedy,* 116;
  and death of God, 58; and life-
  world, 37; and logocentrism,
  125–26; metaphor in, 126–29;
  mythic method of, 117; nemesis of
  being, 16–17; and ontology, 124;
  rhetorical mode of, 126; "Socrates
  and Tragedy," 123; technological
  psychosis in, 6; and wasteland, 78;
  West's last thinker, 5; *The Will to
  Power,* 28
Nihilism, 75; in postmodernism, 2;
  Western thought is, 47
Noema, 23
Noesis, 23
Nothing, 69–70
Noumenon, and earth, 63

Ontological difference, 19, 83
Ontology, rejected, 45

Open, the, 46
Oppositionism, 78, 82, 86
Order, universal, 69
Organism: denial of, 90; myth of, 40; as ultimate reference, 85; as unifying, 85

Paradox: epistemological, 118; at heart of world, 38, 39, 64, 75, 86, 123, 124; of substance, 33, 37, 40, 62, 63, 74
Pascal, Blaise, 47
Peirce, Charles Sanders, 91, 99, 107
Pentad: as being of subject, 40; and Dasein, 37; a generating principle, 34; is interpretation, 61; is Kantian, 39; of key terms, 34; and man, 39; open to history, 36; and paradox of substance, 39; as structure of act, 35; and ten ratios, 34; as transcendental, 39
Perfection, rotten with, 12
Personalism, 50
Personality, principle of, 66, 75
Phenomenology, 21–22
Philosophy: deconstructed, 35; a genre, 130; now ending, 56; option against, 82; as poetic action, 35; supplanted by grammatology, 101
Physics, 7
Piety, 27, 67, 69
Plato, 35, 45, 64, 87
Plotinus, 35, 50, 52, 55
Poet, and logic, 130
Poetic act, as structure, 35
Poetry, destructive, 80
Positivism, 76
Postmodernism: dogmatism of, 86; opposes synthesis, 1
Pound, Ezra, 95
Power: ambient of, 78–79; fantasy of, 79
Presence, 90
Present-at-hand, 38

Pre-Socratics, 4, 51
Proust, Marcel, 105, 106, 131; À la recherche du temps perdu, 113–14
Purpose, 13–14

Rationalism, 4
Ratios, 34, 35
Reader-response theory, 83
Reading, is metaphor, 113
Reality: degradation of, 78; and post-Cartesian thought, 78
Reduction, 21; used by Derrida, 101
Referent, distinguishable, 44
Referentiality: denied by deconstructionism, 96; implicit in de Man, 106
Repetition, of possibility, 80
Resoluteness, 27
Resolve, 48
Revenge, as representative thought, 47
Rhetoric: as deficiency of meaning, 119; new meaning of, 106; tension with grammar, 127; where none exists, 112
Rhetorical mode: compels Nietzsche, 126; is indeterminate, 105
Richardson, Father William J., 64, 65
Ricoeur, Paul, 22
Romanticism, 85, 115
Rorty, Richard, 76
Rousseau, Jean-Jacques, 87

Santayana, George, 40
Sartre, Jean-Paul, 3; and consciousness, 70; and freedom, 13
Saussure, Ferdinand de, 87, 99, 100
Scheler, Max, 21, 59
Schopenhauer, Arthur, 115, 119
Science, and ontology, 74
Semantic ideal, 16
Semiotics, 83
Sense, memories of, 92
Shakespeare, William, 131
Sign: engendered by object, 107–8; in Saussure, 87; and thought, 92

Signified: as signifier, 91; as trace, 97
Sky, 58–59
Socrates, 115, 118
Solipsism, 21; as absolute, 77, 91; of
    Berkeley, 92; in Husserl, 22; a kind
    of, 43; not complete, 44; as scandal,
    22
Sophocles, 115, 127
Space scientists, 75
Speech-act theory, 83, 107, 113
Spinoza, Baruch, 17, 29, 35, 66
Steiner, George, 140n18
Structuralism, 83; a thinking of being,
    76
Structure of becoming, 17–18, 40
Subjectivity, 48
Sublime, 85
Substance, 32; ambiguity in, 38; and
    human relationships, 29–30; para-
    dox of, 33, 37; science of, 40
Super-personality, 85
Synthesis, a gamble, 79

Terministic screens, 29
Terminology, 15
Text, interpretability of, 85
Theoretical knowledge, 38
Theory of ritual, 83
They-world, 25
Thing, the: the being of, 58–63; as
    bridge, 59; ideas lurking in, 62;
    prior to object, 62; sign of words,
    16; as the world, 60
Thinking: of being, 48–56; causal, 4;
    is corresponding, 63; has not be-
    gun, 88; of the heart, 47; a new way

of, 54; nonconceptual, 45; and po-
    etry, 48; representative, 22, 45, 47,
    48; as taking a hand, 63; a thanking,
    47; as thinking being, 47, 65; valu-
    ative, 5
Thought: as autonomous, 7–8, 49;
    means nothing, 88; supplants God,
    8; of the West, 47
Thrownness, 26
Time, as horizon, 24
Todorov, Tzvetan, 106
Trace, 97, 98, 102, 104
Truth, 32, 55
Turn, a, 64

Uncanniness, 26
Undecidables, 97–99; as transcen-
    dentals, 102–4
Ur-Heidegger, 141n26

Vygotsky, Lev, 92

Wagner, Richard, 115, 117, 118; Tris-
    tan and Isolde, 126
Wasteland, 7, 36
Western civilization: deconstruc-
    tionism ends, 77; at end, 88; falla-
    cious, 77
Will, 119–20
Wittgenstein, Ludwig: Tractatus,
    Philosophical Investigations, 15
World, as relationships, 23
Writing, 94–96. See Arche-writing

Yeats, William Butler: "Among School
    Children," 108–9, 111–12

The author acknowledges with thanks the permission granted by the following copyright holders to quote from copyrighted works:

Kenneth Burke: *Attitudes toward History* (copyright 1959), *Permanence and Change: An Anatomy of Purpose* (copyright 1954), both by Kenneth Burke.

Harper & Row, Publishers, Inc.: Martin Heidegger, *Basic Writings* (copyright 1977); *Being and Time* (copyright 1962); *Nihilism*, vol. 4 of *Nietzsche* (copyright 1982); *On the Way to Language* (copyright 1971); *On Time and Being* (copyright 1972); *Poetry, Language, Thought* (copyright 1971); *The Question Concerning Technology* (copyright 1977); *What Is Called Thinking?* (copyright 1968).

Johns Hopkins University Press: Jacques Derrida, *Of Grammatology* (copyright 1976).

Yale University Press: Paul de Man, *Allegories of Reading: Figural Language in Rousseau, Nietzsche, Rilke, and Proust* (copyright 1979).